2

CROSS-COUNTRY MASTERCLASS

with Leslie Law

CROSS-COUNTRY MASTERCLASS

with Leslie Law

DEBBY SLY

David & Charles

A DAVID & CHARLES BOOK

Photographs (unless credited otherwise) by Sue
Williams-Gardner

A catalogue record for this book is available from the
British Library.

ISBN 0 7153 0215 9

Typeset by ABM Typographics Ltd, Hull
and printed in Great Britain by BPC Paulton Books Ltd
for David & Charles
Brunel House   Newton Abbot   Devon

Contents

Introduction

Natural talent and hard work have enabled Leslie Law to make a career out of something most people can only enjoy as a hobby: the sport of eventing. From the yard he and his wife Harriet have set up in Gloucestershire he produces and competes up to fourteen horses, all owned by eventing enthusiasts who do not wish to compete but who enjoy seeing their horses progress through the grades under Leslie's expert guidance.

Leslie's first eventing experience was in the Pony Club, from which he moved on to point-to-point riding for local trainers in Herefordshire. He was then offered a job by Mrs Revel Guest-Albert, who was keen to buy and breed young horses to be sold on as made eventers. She gave Leslie one of his luckiest breaks when she sent him to America to train with Ian Silitch for two years. At that time the American approach to jump training was far more technical than in England; great emphasis was placed on teaching the rider to help his horse by placing him accurately at his fences.

When Leslie returned to England he continued to ride for Mrs Guest-Albert, and was spotted by Sam Barr, breeder of the famous Welton event horses, who subsequently offered him the ride on his stallion Welton Apollo. That was in 1985, and until he rode Apollo, Leslie had only competed at Novice level. He sat on Apollo for the first time the day before he was due to ride him in the Advanced class at Weston Park; they jumped clear to finish seventh. Leslie's dash and determination across country complemented Apollo's laid-back attitude to life, and they were an exhilarating combination to watch. In the five years that Leslie rode him the partnership were only unplaced five times, completed Badminton three times, finishing eighth in 1989, and were twice placed fourth at Gatcombe in the British Open Championship. They also represented Britain at the 1989 European Championships. Apollo retired to stud in 1990.

In 1992 Leslie and Harriet moved to their own yard, Cold Croft Stables. The site is owned by Mr and Mrs Goodwin, whose daughter Leslie had been teaching. They had fifty acres of grazing and an outdoor school, and allowed Leslie and Harriet to build a yard on the farm. The move gave the Laws the chance to attract and retain rides on some very good horses.

The numerous successes that Leslie achieves at all levels, from Novice one-day events to the four-star three-day events, ensure that his name is regularly featured near the top of the event riders' league table, which lists the top hundred riders. As Leslie explains, 'My aim is to carry on competing at as high a level as possible. And to win Badminton, and ride successfully for the British team! Although nothing can be guaranteed with horses I feel that my aims are much nearer being achieved with the good horses and supportive and enthusiastic owners that I now have.'

1 Leslie and His Horses

TYPE AND SUITABILITY

Event horses have to be multi-talented animals: able to move well, and with sufficient obedience to score well in the dressage. They must be careful, agile jumpers for the showjumping, yet bold and fast for the cross-country, able to gallop and jump confidently and safely out of their stride.

'Because of the diverse skills required in eventing, a great many different types of horse can all do equally well overall within the sport. But each will have his good and bad points, and it is the rider's job to balance these out so as to produce a good all-round performer. It is also important to understand and appreciate the horse's attitude and temperament, as well as his good and bad physical points: thus a horse with a really good attitude and temperament but of perhaps moderate physique can

A powerful and honest horse like Haig will never be stretched by the size of a fence but will find some of the twists and turns required at some obstacles harder to cope with

often do a lot better than a more physically talented horse which is perhaps less co-operative. Mental attitude has to be balanced against physical ability.'

'When you buy an event horse you have to consider what you really want to do, and how far you expect to go with that horse. All the horses we have are good event types and I have no problem with riding any of them, but if I was buying one for myself I would always go for the rangier type. Odin's Missile is probably an easier horse to ride, especially for someone who just wants to get to two- or three-star level, as he would be easier to collect up and set up for his fences – because he has a shorter stride he will never be that far off a reasonable take-off point, and would be more able to fiddle his way through a combination if he came in wrong. At four-star level, however, he would find it harder than the more rangy horse to cope with the faster speeds and the bigger fences, and he

would then rely more on his rider to get him into his fences at the right distance so that he could still make the spreads without overstretching himself.

'The rangier horses are not such easy rides at any level as they need more collecting up and organising, but they can gallop and jump for fun. They will find the task easy as long as their rider is capable of balancing them sufficiently in front of the fences.

'So, if you are looking for a horse which will give you experience at two- and three-star level but no higher, you would be better off buying a horse like Odin. But if you want the horse you are buying now to take you to Badminton, then you should go for the rangier type and learn to ride that type of horse.'

On pages 12 and 13 Leslie discusses a selection of the horses he rides, looking at their differing conformation and suitability. Here he discusses in more detail the main horses featured in this book. 'I think Perryfields George has a very exciting future. He came to us as a four-year-old, and it was immediately obvious that he was a very trainable and confident character. He competed successfully in the Burghley Young Event Horse classes before making his debut in horse trials at the age of five (the 1994 season). After a couple of Pre-Novice competitions we tried him at Novice level, which he handled very well; he won two events, after which I began to take him steadier across country to prevent him upgrading too quickly. He finished the season with 16 points. Next year the plan is to do a couple of Novice events and then go on to Intermediate. I would hope to take him to a one- or

two-star three-day event at the end of his six-year-old season. George has progressed exceptionally quickly, partly because physically he is very balanced for a young horse, but mainly because of his temperament. He is very co-operative and is always on your side. He loves his work and he loves to please. I think he has a very big future.

'Cruiseway, or Fatman as he is known at home, is a lovely big horse who has really come into his own this season at the age of six. He came to us as a four-year-old to be broken in, and all we did with him that first summer was quietly ride him out and do a little bit of schooling. We had him back as a five-year-old to do the Burghley Young Event Horse classes and his first Pre-Novice events that autumn, one of which he won. This year he has made even better progress; he's really come to terms with what the sport is all about, and won his last three Novice events, finishing the season as an Intermediate with 30 points. He has an amazing gallop and just loves the cross-country so he should be a real pleasure to ride at a three-day event. If he qualifies in time I hope he will do a two-star three-day event next spring, and depending on how he progresses at that level he will then do either a two- or three-star event next autumn. He is another young horse with great prospects.

'Missy (Best by Miles) started with us in December 1993. She started doing Novice events in the spring as a six-year-old, and has stayed at that level all season. She is ready to upgrade to Intermediate next year, and will hopefully do a two-star three-day event next spring. Mentally and physically she is very energetic and forward going.

This is great for the cross-country phase, but for her dressage and showjumping we need to slow her down and contain her enthusiasm somehow. She is very bold and scopey and has picked up some good placings this year, and with this experience behind her she should go on to greater things as a seven-year-old.

'I have ridden The Magnate now for several years, starting with him as quite an experienced Novice before taking him through Intermediate and then, in 1993, up to Advanced. That year he completed Bramham in the spring; he tried very hard and responded well to all the questions that were asked of him to finish eleventh. I rode him in the Intermediate Championships at Gatcombe, where, as I explain later, he seemed to grow in confidence as he made his way round, and went on to Blenheim three-day event where he finished in the top twenty. He should then have had a go at Badminton in 1994 but sadly, at Blenheim, he damaged his suspensory ligament and had a year off. So now he will probably go back to do another three-star event and Badminton will have to wait until another year.

'Booze Cruise is another lovely young horse who came to me as a seven-year-old in 1993. He had done quite a lot of unaffiliated competitions and so went quickly through Pre-Novice and on to Novice. By the end of his first season he was competing successfully at Intermediate level and rounded off the year by finishing third at Blair Castle CCI**. I had envisaged that he would continue to progress rapidly in 1994, but he had several problems with his feet which have meant a lot of time off, but this seems to have been sorted now. He is very good in all three phases, is very willing to please and is one of the most level-headed horses I have ridden, so his next season should be very exciting.

'I started riding Sidney's King as a seven-year-old in 1993; he is an incredibly bold horse, and so jumping is never a problem to him. His flatwork is improving all the time, but still tends to handicap him; despite this he quickly upgraded to Intermediate and completed Le Lion d'Angers at the end of his first season. In 1994 I brought him out and after a few Intermediates he completed one Advanced before going to Bramham CCI***. He performed really well, going like a machine across country, to finish in the top twenty. He produced a similar performance at Blenheim at the end of the year. If his dressage continues to improve he should be a superb Advanced horse. He is now ready to do Badminton.

'I half-own Welton Envoy with Sam Barr, who bred him, and have ridden him since he was backed as a four-year-old. I rode him quietly through Pre-Novice and Novice as a five-year-old, and as a six-year-old he upgraded to Intermediate. He was slower to adjust to this level than I had expected, but then he was only six and somewhat less mature than I had given him credit for. Because of this he was aimed at a CCI* at the end of his six-year-old season, which he won. In 1994, as a seven-year-old, he has proved himself to be a very successful event horse; he took on the Advanced tracks far better than I had imagined. I assumed he would take time to adjust as he had when he upgraded to Intermediate, but he did not seem to notice the difference at all. He has been placed in all his Advanced competitions; he won the Advanced section at Althorp, and was third in the Intermediate Championships at Gatcombe. He finished the 1994 season off by competing at Le Lion d'Angers CCI**. We had gone out there with very high hopes of winning, but after a good dressage test he struggled to cope with the very deep going. He just seemed to get bogged down in it, and this led to him having a stop going into the water. Although the result was obviously disappointing I was still pleased with his attitude to everything that was asked of him; it was just unfortunate that the ground did not suit him. He is a very trainable horse, and combines very good movement on the flat with a wonderful jumping technique. His next target will be a spring CCI*** and then we will decide whether to go straight to Burghley that same year, or to do another three-star event and aim at Badminton the year after.

'Haig is one of the kindest, nicest horses I have ever ridden. I first rode him when he was nine, and that year he won Windsor CCI** and was then fifth at Boekelo CCI***. We had high hopes of taking him to Badminton as a ten-year-old, but he injured his tendon during his fitness preparation, and it cost him the whole of that season. He is a great big, old-fashioned type of event horse; nothing is too big for him, and it is a wonderful feeling to walk a big track knowing that he is not going to "scope-out" – none of it will stretch him. He should have had another chance at Badminton in 1994 because this time he was fit, but my broken ankle ruled us out. He has had niggling leg and foot problems on and off for the last few years, which always seem to deny him his big moment. After a fantastic performance in the Open Championships at Gatcombe 1994, when he finished fifth, he bruised his sole which denied him the chance of going to Burghley. It is everyone's dearest wish to get him to Badminton if we can; he is such a kind, brave horse he really does deserve a chance to prove himself.'

Leslie and Harriet consider the options at Blenheim's Dew Pond

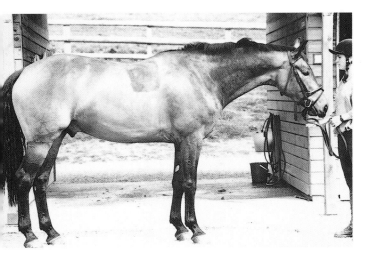

ODIN'S MISSILE: 6 yr old, 16.1hh, ¾ T.B. by Cruise Missile out of a Grade B showjumper

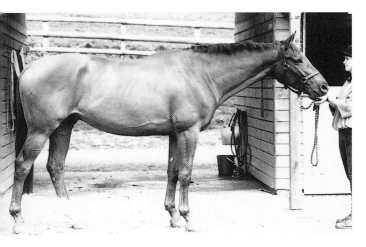

PERRYFIELDS GEORGE: 5 yr old, 16.3hh, T.B. gelding by Itzu

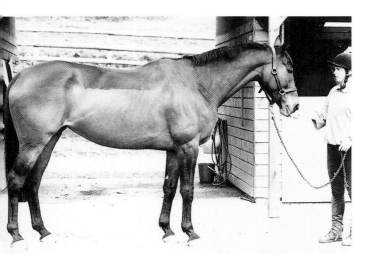

BEST BY MILES: 6 yr old, 16.2hh, T.B. mare by Cruise Missile

Odin's Missile

'Odin is a very short-coupled, chunky sort of horse. He is well proportioned and a very correct type; he has a good shoulder and is put together well. Because of his compact frame he should be quite an easy horse for anyone to ride as he finds it easy to shorten himself, but he wouldn't have the same ground-covering stride that a rangier horse would have when galloping across country.'

Perryfields George

'George is a lovely stamp of a horse; if anything he is fractionally light of bone for his top, but in these pictures he is still carrying a little too much weight; once he is three-day-event fit this would not be so noticeable. He has a super shoulder which allows him to move very well, and a lovely front. He is still a little flat over his rump but this has built up since he was a four-year-old and I would expect it to build up a little more. But from riding him I know that despite this he has a real engine in there. Although he is that much rangier than, say, Odin, because he has so much power behind, he is very light on his feet and finds it easy to collect himself. Despite my slight criticism of his lightness of bone, he is as good a model for an event horse as I have had.'

Best By Miles

'Missy is again on the light side of bone (8½in) but she is not as big-topped as George so she is more in proportion. She is quite long through her back which is not a bad thing in a mare from a breeding point of view, and she again is a very rangy type. She has lovely movement, but does find collection a little harder than the other two would; however, the amount of collection that is required from an event horse is still well within her capability. Because of her build and frame she is a tremendous galloper, as is George. Odin, who could not produce such a gallop, does have the advantage of being easy to collect up again, and therefore will be easier to set up for his fences. Interestingly, Missy and Odin are both by Cruise Missile which just shows how much the dam influences the offspring.

'Personally I prefer to ride the rangier Thoroughbred types like George and Missy because they are real gallopers – their rangy frame might be a handicap in pure dressage, but the degree of collection required in horse trials' dressage is still within their capability so it is less of a handicap than it would be in a horse intended for pure dressage.'

Sidney's King

'Sid is a 16.2hh full Thoroughbred and is, generally, a good model of an event horse. He has a very good shoulder, he looks powerful, and has a very bold eye and expression. He has good limbs and his body is in proportion to his amount of bone. He is fairly straight, however, along his back and spine, and this indicates some stiffness; this also shows in the fact that he lacks muscle along his back and hindquarters. A great deal of his schooling work is aimed specifically at helping him to overcome this stiffness and to build up muscle, so he would do a lot of stretching work. If anything he is a little long in the back, but the overall picture is of a real athlete, complete with jumper's bump! He is also the lean, angular type of horse which recent research has concluded is better able to cope with the heat and humidity so often prevailing at our World and Olympic competitions.'

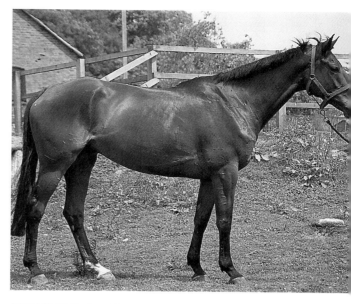

SIDNEY'S KING: 8 yr old, 16.2hh, T.B. by Royal Vulcan

Haig

'Huggy is a big, strong old-fashioned type of event horse, ¾ or ⅞ Thoroughbred, with a really bold outlook and expression. He is a totally different type of horse to Sid, with a much bigger, bulkier body, and a huge front and shoulders. His neck is somewhat light in comparison to the rest of him, but for eventing this doesn't matter as much as it might for, say, pure dressage, because he carries himself well anyway; it comes up and out of his shoulder, too, so the shape is good.

'He is very deep through the girth, has a super angle on his hind legs, and has a really good engine behind. The muscle development over his loins and hindquarters is good, and this shows that he works well on the flat, and really uses his body.

'His forelimbs are somewhat weak in comparison to the weight of his shoulders, and he is very slightly back at the knee. Sadly this predisposes him to tendon strain, as there is too much weight bearing solely on the tendons rather than evenly down the forelimb.

'Although Huggy and Sid are very different to look at, they are both very good Advanced event horses. Haig's power means he will nearly always have a good dressage mark as he has much stronger paces than Sid; but Sid's lightness and athleticism allow you to go faster across country, and he is more likely to stay sound. With Haig you need to be well ahead after the dressage because on the cross-country you will be stuck in a slower – albeit stronger – rhythm than the quick pace you can achieve with Sid. Both horses are tremendously bold, however, and have enormous scope.'

HAIG: 12 yr old, 16.3hh, by Ideal Water out of The Barmaid

13

2 Yard Routine and Fitness

The key to producing a happy and confident competition horse undoubtedly lies in its management at home, and the successful yard is the one which is punctilious in its attention to the feeding, exercise and schooling requirements of the individual horse. The number of good horses entrusted to Leslie and Harriet's care speaks for itself. Here, Leslie describes the daily routine at their Cold Croft yard:

'The horses are fed at 7am, and are given horsehage, fresh water, and the beds are skipped out. If any horse has finished all its water overnight, then it is offered fresh water before its feed. All the horses have two buckets of water at all times.

'Exercising usually starts at 8.30am, and the roadwork and schooling takes until 12.45. In warm weather, the horses are washed down completely after exercise; excess water is drawn off with a sweat scraper, and they are rubbed with towels to dry them off – Harriet calls this the 'feel-good factor'. Special attention is paid to washing and drying the lower legs where boots are worn. The skin needs to be kept very clean otherwise the boots will rub, particularly if you ride on an all-weather surface for much of the time.

'The horses are fed, and given horsehage and fresh water at 1pm; exact feed times are rigorously adhered to. They are then left to rest for an hour before being groomed. Those that have not yet had any time out in the paddock are turned out for an hour or so, and groomed when they come back in. Any medical treatment is given now or before morning exercise; with such a large number of horses there is nearly always one that needs attention. During the afternoon all the routine chores are carried out, such as tack cleaning, mane and tail pulling, trimming and clipping, washing the lorry and so on.

'In summer time the beds are tidied up at 4.30pm, and fresh water is given; haynets go up at 5pm, and the last feed is given at 5.30pm. During the winter the evening hay and feed is given half an hour earlier. Feed buckets are removed as soon as they are empty, and then the horses are left in peace for the evening. In the summer they are not rugged up until about 9.30pm. At 10pm we take a final look round and check on everything before leaving them for the night.

'Although we are always striving to improve our standards, we are happy with the routine we have adopted as the horses seem to thrive on it. The only thing we would change, if we lived on site, would be to feed four times a day; the horse has a small stomach designed to take in feed little and often, so a routine of smaller feeds given more frequently suits its digestive system much better.'

DAILY EXERCISE PROGRAMMES

In Leslie and Harriet's yard the daily exercise requirement for each horse is carefully worked out, each day contributing to the fitness and training schedule preparing him for his particular level of event. For the Novice horses the weekly programme would look like this:

Monday Day off.

Tuesday One hour's hack: hill work mainly walking and trotting. Some horses have 20 minutes schooling and then a 40 minutes hack.

Wednesday Fast work: three times up a $4\frac{1}{2}$ to 5 furlong gallop at Novice cross-country pace. This is to teach the young horse to gallop in a balanced rhythm as much as to get him fit.

Thursday One hour's work: schooling either on the flat or jumping, plus roadwork.

Friday One hour's work: flatwork plus hack.

Saturday If a horse is not competing it will either go for an hour's hack, or be lunged for half an hour in the morning and half an hour in the afternoon.

Sunday Either compete, or go out for an hour's hack, or lunged.

'The Intermediate and Advanced horses will follow the same kind of routine except that they do up to two hours' work each day, to include flatwork, jump schooling and roadwork, always in a carefully worked out programme. Apart from the days that they gallop, they always do 1 to 1½ hours' roadwork. If they are not competing in one particular week then they will be scheduled to do fast work on two days; otherwise it is once a week, with the event counting as the second day of fast work.'

FITNESS

There is little joy, or sense, in riding an unfit horse across country. Part of the thrill of eventing is crossing the country on a fit horse that is keen to gallop, and just eats up the fences as he strides effortlessly round. This happy state can only be achieved by putting in the essential, albeit sometimes tedious, roadwork and fast work that together build up the horse's muscle and strength, and increase his heart and lung capacity. Leslie describes the routine that he and Harriet prefer their horses to follow:

'The horses that are based in our yard all the time are given three to four weeks off after their autumn three-day event. After a spring three-day event they would have two weeks complete rest, and then gentle exercise for two weeks before picking up their usual routine. I don't like any horse to have too much time off work as it loses too much muscle. It used to be standard practice to give horses eight weeks off at the end of the season, but the new thinking is that to have so long not working leads to more injuries.

'So after their autumn three-day event and a three- to four-week rest, we work them gently for, say, just four days a week until we have built up a level of fitness which allows us to take them to the occasional indoor showjumping or dressage competition, or for half a day's hunting, without them having to be in really hard work. This moderate level of fitness is maintained until the New Year, when they will start a full work programme of six days a week.

'Immediately after their rest they do no more than walk for the first ten to fourteen days, after which their roadwork is gradually built up. By the New Year they would be ready to resume their normal exercise routine as by then their muscles would be in good tone. Using this system we seem to avoid the panic that always prevailed if, say, a horse had to have time off due to injury, or if the weather conditions limited what you could do.

'By the first week of February we start fast work again, gently to begin with, just a canter on May Hill twice a week, usually up four to five furlongs in no more than a strong working canter. This would be for two to three weeks, and then we would take the Intermediate and Advanced horses to the all-weather gallop that we use locally, which is about seven furlongs all uphill. The surface is simply rotavated sandy soil, and it really makes a horse work but without jarring him up. For the first two weeks they would run up this twice, and after that they go up three times. By the start of the eventing season they would be travelling up this at what we would call their "cruising speed", indicating a state of fitness whereby they can cover the ground at speed but smoothly and without undue exertion; as a horse gets fitter and stronger, his cruising speed will increase.

'To begin with the horses walk all the way back down between gallops; by the middle of the season, however, we would walk and trot them back down to the bottom of the gallop, before letting them run back up again. The aim is to keep the heart and respiration rate up before the horse gallops again, so that each time he has to exert himself a little more, and it is this that builds up the heart and lung capacity.

'When a horse has his first few gallops you will feel him "stretch his girth", or blow out against your legs, about halfway up the gallop – it is then that he gets his second wind. A useful guide is that as the horse gets fitter he should increase the distance covered before he needs his second wind. Also, as fitness increases the horse should still be travelling well when he reaches the top of the

gallop, and not be trying to pull himself up which he will do when he first starts fast work. These are two good reasons why you should always try to use the same gallops.

'When the horse starts fast work it is important that he is not over-stressed. The very first run up should be slow enough so that the horse still reaches the top without struggling too much. This sort of pace should allow you to complete two runs up the gallops, and according to how the horse copes with that, you must then judge how much you can pick up the pace next time. The main thing is never to do too much too soon, and the best way to judge what this really means is to look at the gallop and think what *you* would do if you were asked to run up it; I bet you would start off fairly steadily until you knew exactly how much effort was involved in getting up there once, and how much it would take out of you! Only once you knew what was involved, and as you got fitter, might you be prepared to start off faster!

'It does help to work some horses together, as they seem to draw inspiration and encouragement from company. The only time I would gallop a horse on its own is one that is very strong and excitable, such as Sidney's King; his sort I would want to teach to gallop in a rhythm but without pulling against me all the time in an effort to go faster and faster.'

FEEDING

'The main aim of our feeding regime is to provide a well balanced diet, and we like to keep to a strict routine with regard to feeding times. The hard feed rations we usually give, in varying quantities, are a mixture of coarse mix, oats and sugar beet, and we add extra roughage and bulk in all the feeds; this may be in the form of high fibre Hi Fi which only contains a small amount of alfalfa, and then horses competing at three- and four-star level are given Alfa A, which is mollassed alfalfa, instead of Hi Fi. The Novice horses have mainly coarse mix and sugar beet unless they tend to be fat, in which case some of the coarse mix will be replaced by oats, and they will get less sugar beet. The amount of sugar beet given in each feed varies from a small handful to half a scoop.

'The amount of feed given varies according to each horse, and is dictated by how that horse looks and feels, and how he is coping with his work. What we do feel very strongly is that each feed should contain the same mix of ingredients, so that the horse's stomach is always acclimatised to what he is given, and can therefore digest it readily. So we would not give all the oats in one feed, and then all the coarse mix in the next – each feed contains all the different ingredients that we wish that horse to receive: the quantity and sometimes the proportions may vary, but not the nature of its contents.

'The average quantities of hard feed – concentrates – we might feed to horses at different levels are these: the Novices, 6 to 8lb; the Intermediates, 8 to 10lb; and the Advanced horses, 10 to 14lb. All the horses in our yard have certain supplements in their evening feed, namely half a teaspoon of limestone flour, a tablespoon of vegetable oil, garlic and salt. The Intermediate and Advanced horses are given Red Cell, which is an iron and vitamin B supplement, and seaweed is given to any horse with a poor coat, skin or feet. We also provide electrolytes in very hot weather, when the horses will be sweating a lot; for the rest of the time sugar beet is a good source of electrolytes anyway.

'Horsehage is fed in proportion to concentrate feed, thus in general the more hard feed a horse receives, the less hay we give him, unless we are trying to put weight on him – though having said that, we never feed less than 30 per cent roughage in the diet otherwise the horse's gut stops functioning properly. So a three-day-event horse would probably be on a ration of 70 per cent concentrates to 30 per cent hay, whereas the Novices are usually on 60 per cent concentrates to 40 per cent hay, or sometimes even 50:50.

'We try to maintain a dust-free environment so the hay is either soaked, or we buy haylage. We feed in bowls on the ground, and these are removed as soon as they are empty, and then cleaned. We prefer to use buckets for water, rather than automatic drinkers, so that we know as soon as a horse isn't drinking its usual amount.

'When the horses are rested at the end of the season, or after an event, we continue feeding them; the hard feed is gradually reduced and the amount of hay increased until they are on a ration of 30 per cent concentrates to 70 per cent hay.'

TACK AND EQUIPMENT

'I like to keep tack and equipment as simple as possible. I generally compete in a snaffle, which may range from a thick German eggbutt to a French link. We use either cavesson or flash nosebands for all the disciplines, and rarely have them fitted tight. Too many people are too quick to strap their horses' mouths shut when it isn't necessary, and this can often cause more resistances than it cures. If I need to ride something in a martingale at home then I use a standing martingale; it is completely independent of the rider's hand, and only comes into effect when the horse throws his head up too high; I may also use one when I showjump indoors during the winter. At a BHS horse trials a standing martingale is not permitted, and so if a horse really needs something in the showjumping then I do use a running martingale; as a safety precaution I always ride in a running martingale on the cross-country phase. We use rubber-covered reins for jumping, and when a running martingale is worn, we use two rubber stops on each rein, one each side of the martingale rings.

'At home I don't bother with a breastplate as it can rub the horse, but one is always put on at an event. I personally prefer a breastplate to a breastgirth which I think can be a bit restrictive.

'For saddles the ideal situation is when each horse would have its own saddle, but because of the number of horses in the yard we cannot do this. So

I have two jumping and two dressage saddles, and they have to be used for everything; it isn't ideal, but is more realistic in our situation. Because we only have four saddles between about fourteen horses, we put a lot of padding underneath them to make sure they don't rub, or lie too high or low on the withers. We like leather girths, and numnahs that are made of natural materials such as cotton or sheepskin; it is important to make sure that the numnah fits the saddle you are using. We are always on the lookout for anything that might be rubbing or pinching. For cross-country riding we use a surcingle, or overgirth, to help secure the saddle.

'We attach great importance to keeping all the tack and equipment as clean as possible; in general, the better the condition it is in, the less likely it is to rub or break! Regular checks are made to all stitching and buckles.

'Boots and bandages are all part of the "uniform" nowadays, and at home we generally use Woof boots; but if any horse has got a rub of any sort then we use exercise bandages and fibregee. Boots very soon start to rub if you are working in a sand school, or if the horse sweats a lot. We use overreach boots on any horse that needs them.

'When showjump schooling at home we might use open-fronted boots in front and fetlock boots behind; these would be the same as we use at a competition, so that the horses don't get careless. For fast work we use the same boots or bandages as we do for the cross-country. We find the "Style" boots very good as they have a good tendon shield but are still very light, and they don't retain water. If we use bandages then we put Porter boots underneath rather than just fibregee, and we would cut the tapes off and either use velcrose or stitching. To bandage a horse properly takes a certain amount of time and concentration, and with the number of horses we are dealing with it is easier, quicker, and therefore probably safer to use boots. Overreach boots are always worn for galloping and cross-country.

'We only put in studs if the going warrants it, generally when the ground is very hard or greasy. In deep going, or in perfect going we would not use them at all. We would have road studs in front – ideally two, so as not to unbalance the foot – and then one stud behind, on the outside edge of the shoe; on hard ground this will be a pointed stud, for greasy going it would be a blunter, chunkier stud.'

INJURIES

'Observation is one of the best ways of preventing injury. Notice how a horse moves, so that you can put on protective boots or bandages if he knocks himself in any way; know each horse well so that if you observe any change from the norm in a horse's well-being and behaviour you can be ready to take action. When it comes to treatment, there are so many restrictions now on what painkilling substances it is safe to use so you can still compete, that if you can find a herbal or homœopathic remedy that works then there is a lot less to worry about.

'Try E45 cream to help prevent rubs; we put it on under the horses' boots at events, and at home on anything with particularly sensitive skin. At three-day events and at Advanced one-day events the horses have cross-country grease smeared over their legs, on the forelegs all down the front, and also the backs of the knees and the fetlock joints. Behind, it goes all the way down from the stifle to the coronet, and on the back of the fetlock joints.

'Sheepskin covers are used on girths and on breastplates if the horse has sensitive or rubbed skin.

'Bits are kept scrupulously clean, otherwise the build-up of dirt will rub the sides of the mouth. If any horse has a sore mouth, which can happen if it pulls very hard across country, we use bit guards, or ride in a hackamore.

'For minor cuts Tea Tree cream, available from any chemist, is a very good antiseptic healing cream; there is also Kaltostat, a seaweed gauze which helps prevent proud flesh and encourages skin tissues to heal very quickly without granulating.

'We are constantly on the watch for any sign of knocks or sprains, and would rather prevent than have to cure: thus after the cross-country phase of a three-day event, after galloping at home, or if we know a horse has had a knock, we get ice onto the legs as quickly as possible; it should be applied for 10 to 15 minutes every 2 to 3 hours. A quick and easy way to apply ice to the leg is to damp and freeze sheets of gamgee, which you can then mould around the legs and bandage in place. We always use this at home after galloping, as it brings down any swelling but without masking any major injury which may have occurred.

'Arnica is an important component of our medicine cupboard: we take this ourselves, in tablet form, and give it to any horse that is doing a three-day event, or has had a stressful one-day event, or has been injured or traumatised in any way.'

3 Ground Rules for Cross-Country Riding

'For me, the thrill of cross-country riding is in always getting to the other side, of accomplishing successfully the challenge that has been set by the course designer, and the real buzz comes from riding a horse which you feel is doing the job properly and is enjoying it. I really don't enjoy taking a bad horse round, nor is simply jumping the fastest clear necessarily very satisfying – I would get more enjoyment from a steadier round on a better horse. Persuading a horse to jump round well and confidently shows that you have done a good job in training him at home, and that he trusted you sufficiently to perform well on the day. I am only happy if the performance has felt right – that is where the real fulfilment of cross-country riding lies for me.

'For it all to come right it is vital to have a horse that is capable of giving you that feel, and some horses simply cannot, no matter how much training or work is put into them. The 'right feel' is made up of several things: confidence, because you both must have confidence and trust in each other; honesty, which is the rider knowing that the horse can and will try for him; and a good jumping technique from the horse – he should elevate his shoulders and be round through his back. He should feel like an athlete, and know how to use himself over a fence so that you are really conscious of the power as he comes off the floor; it should feel as if he is punching off the floor so that his withers shoot up to meet your chest.

'There are always exceptions and some horses will never give you that "wow" feeling, but they are wonderful servants and do you well. They make up for their lack of technique with tremendous bravery, and ideally you want a balance of technique and courage. Sidney's King, for example, will never give you a wonderful feeling over a fence but he has tremendous power and courage. Haig, on the other hand, has an excellent technique, as well as courage and scope to spare.

'However, training can play a large part in the sort of feel and performance you do attain from your particular horse, and you can nearly always improve on what you have; but the horse must have some ability and a degree of courage and technique. Also, you can train a horse to give you the "feel" I have talked about, but only if the horse has a feel for training; therefore two horses can have the same training and they will both improve, but one horse will come out a better horse than the other one.

'Cross-country riding involves taking a well-trained athlete from A to B and coping with everything that lies in between, and so the key to successful cross-country riding lies in the training of both the horse *and* the rider. Nor should the significance of flatwork be underestimated in a horse's preparation for cross-country jumping: schooling a horse on the flat is all about creating and maintaining rhythm and balance, and controlling speed and pace, and so dressage training is just as important as jump training if you want to produce a good cross-country horse.

'You can take this several steps further, too: for example when you are giving a horse his gallop work as part of his fitness programme, use it to get a feel for riding in a rhythm – and practise "setting the horse up" on the flat, that is, learning how to steady the horse whilst also keeping the engine running, so that you elevate the front end and get his hocks underneath him as you would when approaching a fence.'

FLATWORK

'As far as I am concerned, the horse's canter is the most important pace to improve for jumping; a good canter is vital. When I ride a horse for the first time it is its canter I am interested in – you can trot around endlessly and appreciate the horse's rhythm and balance in this pace, but that doesn't tell you how easy or difficult he will find jumping – that comes down to how good his canter is.

'In general though, the rider's aim should be to keep the horse in a balanced rhythm in all paces, encouraging him to take the contact forwards politely, and in a nice outline. The correct way of going is helped by using stretching exercises to encourage the muscles on the top line to stay supple, so that when the horse is picked up and asked to work with engagement and in a shorter outline and to stay light in front, the muscles are in better shape to cope with this. Be sure that when the horse stretches down he is round and pushing through from behind; if he is hollow then he is not using these muscles properly. The aim is to stretch the muscles so that when the horse is asked to carry himself in a shorter outline, the muscles respond to this without becoming tight and uncomfortable. If the horse is always worked in a short outline, with the muscles tight and contracted, then he will become stiff, and his paces will look stilted. Stretching also encourages the horse to take the contact forwards and down.

'In short, for both dressage and jumping, the rider should be constantly seeking to develop the horse's suppleness and rhythm, the engagement of his hindquarters and the lightness of his forehand.

'A typical flatwork session for us at home starts with ten minutes walking on a loose rein, and then five minutes "stretching", with the horse working in a long, low, but round outline. During this work we keep changing the rein and turning, and would finish up by cantering, with my weight off the horse's back, while still asking him to stretch down. I then pick the horse up and work on a series of transitions: walk to trot, trot to walk, walk to canter, trot to halt and so on.

'Lengthening and shortening the stride within the pace, in both trot and canter, is a very good exercise. Slowing the horse right down in canter, for just a few strides, teaches him to balance and carry himself; offer him a lighter contact when he does this, before sending him on again. Lengthening and shortening the stride in canter is very beneficial for jumping, as this is something you are doing all the time on the approach to a fence. It teaches the horse to come back in canter with a supple poll and back, without resisting or hollowing against the rider's hand which would then produce a flat jump.

'In all this work the horse must learn to move away from your leg as soon as it is applied; thus leg-yielding is a good test of a horse's obedience to the leg. At all times I insist that the horse is straight, and test this by riding plenty of straight lines, squares and rectangles instead of always working on a circle. If you make sure that the shoulders are straight it is more likely that the hindquarters will then follow through straight; so correct the front (the shoulders) before trying to straighten the quarters.

'All horses are heavier on one rein, in the same way that people are stronger down one side than the other. It is important to strive for evenness in both reins, and it is worth remembering that the horse can only remain heavier in one hand if the rider allows him to; if you keep offering him the rein, or shake him off it when he takes too much of a hold, then he is forced to even himself up. An even contact is as important for jumping as it is for dressage, as it encourages the horse to take off over a fence by pushing equally off both hindquarters; then he will stay straight and get as much height as possible. So if the horse leans on one rein, the rider must work to achieve a stronger contact in the opposite rein (the light rein), and to lighten the contact in the heavy rein. He does this by keeping a constant, firm, but elastic feel in the light rein, and by offering the rein to the horse on his heavy side – when you offer him the rein he can no longer lean on it.

'If the horse tilts his head, nine times out of ten if you do the opposite to what you think is logical – if you take a stronger contact in the rein he is tilting *towards* – then he will probably straighten out. This is because generally the horse tilts his head towards the rein he wants to evade. Another point worth remembering is that evenness of the rein is relative to the activity of the opposite hindquarter; thus if a horse is very light in the right rein, he is probably weak in the left hindquarter. The horse's teeth and mouth must also be checked if he has persistent problems about accepting the contact.

'All the above flatwork training must be established in the Novice horse; once it is, he is ready to move on to anything you like – shoulder-in, quarters-in, counter-canter, medium trot and canter, rein-back and so on. And, once *these* movements are established, as they need to be in the Intermediate horse, the horse's education can progress further to Advanced work: half-pass, medium and extended trot and canter, ten-metre circles etc. It is often quite hard for a horse to balance himself at first on a ten-metre circle, so reduce the circle size gradually, going from twenty to fifteen, and then down to ten for just one or two circles, before leg-yielding away again.

'For jumping, it is important always to work towards improving the canter. I now work the horses in a much rounder canter before I jump them to make sure everything is soft and supple; though when I actually start jumping I don't like the horse to be too round coming into the fence, but prefer him to be elevated in front and light on his forehand. As he comes to a fence he must be able to lower his head and neck in order to use himself properly over the fence – but he can only do this to good effect if he is light in front. If he is on his forehand and leaning on your hand coming into the fence, and you soften the hand so that he can lower his neck, he will practically fall on his face. You must teach the horse to carry himself, and if he learns to come into his fences in this way then you won't have to fight with him in front of a fence in an effort to balance or lighten him. If he carries himself, then you can maintain the rhythm, balance and softness all the way to the fence and then everything improves.

'A tired horse – which he is quite likely to be towards the end of a cross-country course – will start to lean on the rider's hands and go down on his forehand, and that is why, at this stage, the rider has to work even harder to keep him light in front and help him to his fences.'

SOME SCHOOLING EXERCISES

Harriet is responsible for much of the flatwork schooling, and here considers some of the basic principles and how she tries to establish a good way of going in a horse. She discusses work that she and Leslie consider to be directly relevant to jumping: as Leslie says, 'When I come down to a fence I want to be able to close the hand and leg to lighten the horse's front end, and then ride him forwards up to it. I like to be able to do this with a young horse on the flat first of all – I need to feel able to shorten his stride in canter so as to lighten his forehand, and then ride him forwards again without him losing his balance – because only then do I feel confident about riding him across country.'

'The horse is beginning to use himself through his top line, and is stretching forwards into the contact. He is starting to engage his hocks by bringing them well underneath his body so that they start to carry his weight. Stretching work is always done in a steady, but forward rhythm with the horse swinging loosely through his back. He must not be allowed to run on, otherwise his hocks will be left trailing behind him and he will simply be pushing himself on to his forehand.'

◀ Harriet is riding the six-year-old Cruiseway. 'We always begin schooling on the flat with some stretching exercises. I am opening the inside hand to encourage the horse to reach forwards and take the contact down, so that he stretches through his neck and back.'

'After five or ten minutes of stretching work in trot, we go forwards into canter, riding in the half-seat – with just half of your weight in the saddle. Encourage the horse to continue to stretch down if he will, whilst still maintaining the contact.'

'The horse's hocks are still trailing behind him, but he is drawing the contact down in a long and low outline which will help his back end to engage once he has learnt to trust the rider's hand. The horse has to learn that it is good if he takes the contact forwards and down, but he must also learn to trust the contact when the rider tries to pick him up again in order to engage the back end.'

'As we come back down to trot I use this opportunity to shorten the reins. By doing this, and by keeping the leg on, you push the horse up into a more advanced outline. The aim is to try to keep the same contact and feel in the reins as you had in the stretching work, but to encourage the horse to begin to lighten his front end, bring his hocks underneath him, and present a rounder outline.'

Developing the correct outline

'A more advanced outline is achieved by asking the horse to transfer his weight from his front end to his back end. The term "picking the horse up" does *not* mean pulling him together with the hand: the horse has to start this transfer by allowing the rider's leg to push his hocks further underneath him. The stretching work will have activated the muscles in the back and hindquarters and it is important to keep the activity that this work created. I do this by slowing down the pace but increasing the length of stride; this encourages the horse to step further under himself with the hind legs, and then in order to lengthen the stride in front he has to free his shoulders and let the stride develop through them. You can then lighten the contact and ride him forwards again from the leg. This encourages him to carry himself in the correct outline without relying on the rider's hand to hold him up together: the hand should merely guide him and regulate the pace. The rider should always be encouraging him to accept and take the contact forwards by ensuring his hands keep an elastic contact with the horse's mouth.

'Throughout all the horse's work, try to maintain the same feel so as not to complicate things for him. To slow down the trot, think about increasing the weight in the rein, and then decrease the weight when you want him to go forwards again with a longer stride. A good way to think about maintaining the right contact is to imagine holding hands with someone. Riding with one hand – as discussed a little later – really makes you aware of how little or how much hand you have been using.

'As a rider, you must establish on which rein the horse finds it easier to work – he will be "heavier" on one than on the other. Work towards helping him to trust the lighter rein and take more contact on it, and to lean less heavily on the other rein. Try to encourage a really good, consistent contact on the light rein, and give and take the heavier rein to prevent the horse leaning on it, all the while insisting that he stays straight. It is easy to forget about straightness as so much time is spent schooling on a circle, and so it is a good idea to work on straight lines, squares and rectangles too.

'Besides the schooling work we have discussed, other exercises should be introduced such as leg-yielding and shoulder-in, depending on the horse's stage of training.'

INTRODUCING TRANSITIONS

'To further the objective of increasing the activity of the hind end and the freedom of the shoulders, we next introduce transitions, both within the pace, and between paces. In downward transitions we just use a little outside rein to slow the horse. All these exercises are beneficial because they engage the horse's hind end in a completely natural way.'

'Shortening and lengthening the trot is another very helpful exercise: in the first picture I am taking a stronger feel in both reins to slow the trot and shorten the steps whilst trying to maintain the same rhythm. I then ask the horse to lengthen his stride, the aim being that he maintains his balance and the rhythm in doing so.'

'We use the same exercise in canter, and as the horse is asked to lengthen he should do so by raising his shoulder as well as stretching forwards; then the stride will have lift as well as length.'

'Check that you are not using too much hand, and that you have an even rein contact, by putting the reins in one hand; this ensures that you are not holding the horse's head down and in. By dropping one hand you then have to ride more from the leg, and this horse is obviously responding by gradually elevating his front end. At this stage, what we are striving for is evident: the hocks are engaged, and the stride is coming up through a free shoulder so that the front end is more elevated.'

◀ 'As the horse comes back to trot you can see the improvement in his stride; he is really swinging through his back.'

Relaxation periods

'At intervals throughout these training sessions the horse should be allowed to stretch down and take the contact forwards again; this gives his muscles a chance to relax, and he can start to unwind. We always finish off our training sessions by doing this. Cruiseway has very good muscle development for a young horse, so in fact this kind of work is not too difficult for him. Yet some horses could take no more than five or ten minutes work in a correct outline, before needing to stretch down in order to relax and rest their muscles. These periods of relaxation are vital, because if you overwork the horse and do not give him these breaks then he will start to tense up his muscles and this in itself will prevent him working through properly; and he will also start to find ways of resisting or evading you because he is not comfortable.'

CROSS-COUNTRY TECHNIQUE FOR THE RIDER

Rider position

between fences 'A strong lower leg position is essential, both for maintaining your position between fences, as you have to gallop with your seat out of the saddle, and also to enable you to keep a correct, secure position over a fence.

'When galloping between fences it is important to stay in balance with the horse without using the reins or your seat for support; your weight should be out of the saddle so the horse can bowl along underneath you with a long, free stride. The shorter your stirrup length, the easier it is to maintain the correct position on the flat as well as over the fences. The best National Hunt jockeys demonstrate this very well, and anyone who is offered the chance to ride racework should grab the opportunity; it teaches you to stay in balance with a fast, galloping Thoroughbred, it teaches you to judge pace, how to balance and hold a fit, strong horse, and helps get you fit as well. Better still, do some point-to-point riding! Anything like that is invaluable experience, and is bound to help sharpen your reactions.

'When the horse is galloping, the rider's bodyweight should be balanced over the horse's centre of gravity, the withers, and really the only way to learn how it should feel is to go and do it. When you are in balance with the horse your body will remain still as the horse moves underneath you; only your arms will move to follow the contact, as the horse uses his head and neck a great deal at this pace. If your weight is too far forwards you will keep pitching forwards and will end up balancing yourself with your hands on the horse's neck; in this position your weight is in your knees rather than down in your heels. If your weight is too far back, your seat will keep hitting the back of the saddle. Once you can feel your weight down in your heel and can keep your body still, you will know you are in balance. In practice it usually means having your shoulders a lot further forwards than you might imagine is necessary. To find out for yourself though, you do just have to go and do it, and riding racework really is the best way. Most people have a racing or point-to-point yard nearby, and provided you are willing to ride for the experience rather than for cash, it is just a case of going and asking.

'Another way to improve your strength and balance is by trying to hold yourself in the "gallop" position while the horse is trotting along on a hack; you will learn to absorb the horse's movement down through the knees and heels, and the exercise will also help strengthen the leg muscles. Also, as the horse does his gallop work as part of his fitness training, vary your stirrup length: first ride at your normal cross-country length, then pull your stirrups right up short and gallop in that position. If a horse tends to pull, the shorter you ride the easier it is to hold him. And never underestimate how tiring it is to ride with your weight out of the saddle – you do need plenty of strength in your lower leg!'

on the approach: 'Your position as you approach a fence does depend on the type of obstacle in front of you; if it is a straightforward galloping fence you would just allow your upper body to come back a bit, and lower your seat down to the saddle. You should be able to stay in the same rhythm and just open the stride up or shorten it a fraction to meet the fence well. If you also balance the horse a little with your hand as your weight comes back into the saddle you will automatically shorten the stride slightly and lift the horse off his forehand. You then just stay like that all the way to the fence, or open up the stride, if necessary, to make the distance.

'Coming to a coffin or combination fence you need to sit deeper into the saddle to shorten and collect the stride to a much greater degree. You sink your weight deeper into your lower leg and heel, and sit into the saddle; you adopt much more of a showjumping canter, in terms of balance and pace, and rider position. It is important to learn to do this by using your legs and your body position, rather than simply trying to haul the horse up together

to maintain the contact rather than throw the reins at the horse; if you can keep an elastic feel on his mouth it will give him security and support if needed. This is particularly important if the horse pecks, or if he deviates from his line on landing; in a cross-country combination with just a stride or two between elements it is crucial to have the contact intact when landing over the first part so that you can immediately balance and steer the horse through.

'Learning to follow the contact does require practice; you need to have attained an independent seat so that you don't rely on your hands and the reins to balance yourself – they are there to balance the horse! A happy medium has to be found; it is kinder to the horse to over-release with the hands to give him complete freedom over the fence, but it is safer for you and the horse to maintain the contact through the air as long as you don't get left behind and catch him in the mouth.'

▲

with your hands; doing that will mean the horse certainly slows down, but he will lose impulsion and power, his hocks will be trailing behind him, he will drop on his forehand and will probably resist the uncomfortable pulling at his mouth by sticking his head up – all in all he will be worrying more about what you are doing to him, than what he is about to jump. Loss of focus, concentration and balance invariably means at best an uncomfortable jump for both of you, and at worst a refusal or a fall.'

in the air: 'The lower leg needs to stay still and firm, and close to the horse's sides; it should not swing back, as then the weight tips forwards and you are vulnerable to a fall. The upper body should fold forwards from the waist, but only when the horse has actually taken off over the fence, not before. As you fold, allow the hands to follow the contact as the horse stretches his head and neck forwards as he goes through the air. You should try

▼

on landing: 'As the horse starts to land over the fence, open up the upper body by raising the shoulders so that your weight is not loaded on the horse's shoulders. The aim is to keep the seat close to the saddle, but without interfering with the horse's balance – you shouldn't be sitting heavily in the back of the saddle, nor should you suddenly bring your weight down into it. By raising your shoulders as the horse lands, you are in fact using your weight to help keep him off his forehand so that as soon as he lands he is able to stride forwards

▼

immediately. As his hind legs touch down, have the weight well down in the lower leg so that you can "pick him up" straightaway, closing your legs on the girth and asking him to gallop away from the fence.

A surprising amount of time is lost across country by having a laborious landing and a slow getaway from each fence.

'All this organisation of weight and position helps develop the smooth, efficient technique that we are looking for: the ability to jump and land in balance with the horse, with the upper body elevated and the lower leg firmly on the girth so that you can immediately begin to lighten the horse's forehand. In the same way as when approaching a straightforward fence, there should be very little to do, or at least that is the way it should appear; you should lower yourself down into the saddle, elevate your upper body, and balance the horse with your hands and lower leg.

'Watch the good National Hunt jockeys: they demonstrate this smooth, efficient technique time and time again – but then, they can nearly all see a distance to a fence, and they know whether they need to lengthen or shorten the horse's stride to help him meet the fence at a reasonable take-off point; and there is no doubt that if a rider has this ability it is far easier to demonstrate a good technique across country. The good race jockeys always make a decision one way or the other: they either let the horse run on in his stride, or lengthen to the fence, or they crouch down behind him knowing that he is going to shorten his stride and get deep into the fence.'

Quick exercises to help improve the leg position

Heels down: Stand on some steps with your toes on the edge of one step and your heels resting on the step below. This really stretches the muscles down the back of your legs.

Strengthening the lower leg: Hack out with your stirrups extra short whenever possible. More time is generally spent schooling on the flat than over fences, so a lot of time is spent riding at dressage length. Try hacking out shorter even than your jumping length to improve your balance and to strengthen your muscles.

Rider Position

'Safe and enjoyable cross-country riding depends very much on the rider developing a secure position when jumping. A common error is for the rider to anticipate when the horse is going to jump and to start to tilt his body forwards, and to lift his seat out of the saddle before the horse has taken off. This puts him "in front of the movement" and leaves him vulnerable to being unseated should the horse either put back down again and stop, or if it hits the fence. Everybody tends to develop his or her own particular style, but the following qualities are important in all cross-country riding:

'First, to develop as strong and secure a lower leg position as possible. Keep the weight well down in the heel and the lower leg pushed slightly forwards, whilst keeping it closed on the horse's girth.

'Keep your seat as close to the saddle as possible. Give the horse the freedom to jump by folding from the waist and allowing your arms to stretch forwards. Try to imagine that the horse's wither is coming up to meet you, rather than throwing yourself forwards to meet it.

'Concentrate on looking up and ahead always. Where a rider is looking has a great influence not only on his balance and position, but also on what the horse does.

'Never jump before the horse! In other words, don't anticipate and get in front of the horse on take-off. Sit deep in the saddle and keep the shoulders up until the front feet leave the ground. If you find this difficult, think of "crouching down" behind the horse's neck on the last few strides. This should help keep your seat in the saddle and, quite often, having something else to think about is enough to stop you anticipating what is going to happen anyway. Suddenly it just happens.

'In the lower sequence of photos my position looks secure throughout the approach and over the jump. My seat barely comes out of the saddle over the fence, and it certainly stays in the saddle on the approach, and my lower leg is firm and secure throughout, with the heel well down.

'In the other photo sequence Laser has started to apply the brakes in front of this trakehner, and it is in this sort of situation that the rider is pushed in front of the movement as a result of the force with which the horse tries to pull up. My heel has just started to creep up, my shoulders have tilted forwards, and my seat is starting to lift out of the saddle. In the last picture my lower leg has slipped back and I have got "in front of the movement". This often happens, because the rider tries to use his own weight to "lift" the horse over the fence – but it does leave him in a vulnerable position, which is not what you want, particularly in a situation like this where the horse has considered stopping.'

EARLY JUMP TRAINING

Horse and rider can improve their balance by working through grids; gridwork helps the horse's balance and technique as well as teaching the rider to stay in balance with the horse.

Schooling over related-distance fences at home will improve both your showjumping *and* your cross-country riding. For example, if you set up two fences on a tight four-stride distance you will learn the degree of balance and pace that you need from a particular horse to get four even strides between the fences. Open up the distance and practise riding four long strides, feeling the change in balance and pace needed to ride the longer distance.

Schooling exercises at home should be smaller, simpler versions of what you will find on the cross-country course. Riding over 'showjump' versions of typical cross-country combinations helps instil confidence in horse and rider so they can tackle whatever they come across at an event.

With all these types of fence it is important to start very small and build them up, so that the horse grows in confidence at every stage. Ultimately they should be built up to a reasonable height, but very few people jump as high at home as they have to at a competition. Anyway, if the horse is happy about the question he is being asked, then the height of the fence is not that important. For example at Windsor three-day event, one of the most influential combinations used to be fences 5 and 6, two angled logs, which were probably the smallest fences on the course but they were set at about one-and-a-half strides apart. Some horses took one stride and used the half stride to nip out to the side, while others put in two strides, found themselves too close to the second log and stopped. But if you practise over angled fences at home, and gradually make the angles steeper and steeper, you learn how much you can trust your horse and can therefore work out the line through the two fences you must ride in order to achieve a one- or a two-stride distance successfully. With this experience in your mind, this sort of fence is not so much of a problem.

A simple guideline is therefore to school at home over what you might expect to find at a competition. You will have to visit a proper cross-country schooling course to gain experience over water, drops and ditches, but otherwise it is quite possible to reproduce most things at home. Hunting should not be overlooked, either, as an excellent exercise for horse and rider, particularly in its capacity to instil rhythm and balance as you cross all kinds of country.

Gridwork Distances

'In general we use gridwork to encourage the horse to find jumping easy, and to give him confidence when he is faced with a line of fences at a competition,' explains Leslie. 'You see so many horses making mistakes when they come into the showjumping arena, and in both jumping phases horses can be seen chipping in strides or refusing in a combination because they are not adapting to the distances they have been given.

'Working through grids gives us the chance to study the straightness and technique of each horse. If a horse has a particular problem, or if we feel he would benefit from more gymnastic exercises, then he would do gridwork twice a week until we were happy that some improvement had been made. But normally we would give each horse one gridwork session per week.

'The main aim is to prepare the horse for anything he is likely to meet at an event, and to improve his technique, attitude and style in general. An advantage of grids is that, set up correctly, the risk of hurting or frightening the horse is minimal. The rider also benefits by being able to concentrate solely on his own position and style once the horse is on his way up the grid.

'With the younger horses the main aim is to teach the horse to stay straight and in a rhythm, and to use himself over a fence. As a general guide, the distances first used in a grid are as follows:

Placing pole: 8 to 9 feet from the fence.
Landing or canter pole: 9 to 10 feet from the fence.
A bounce from trot: 3 to 4 yards.
Bounce from canter: 4 to 4½ yards.
One-stride distance approached from trot: 6 yards.
One-stride distance from canter: 6½ to 8 yards.

'The distance you start with in a grid should always be one that suits the individual horse's stride. We tend to keep the distance shorter than the standard showjumping one-stride distance (8 yards) to teach a horse to be neat and quick with his front legs. We really put this to the test with some horses by jumping three low but wide oxers all set on 6½-yard distances; this is hard work for them, but it does teach them to use themselves.

'Once a horse is going through a grid confidently on distances which suit him, you can then play around with the measurements to bring about the improvement you are looking for. If the horse is very bold, for example, start with a longer distance, say a bounce of 12 feet, and then work it back gradually to, say, 10 feet, to teach the horse to stay short and contained. If he needs to learn to stretch himself a bit, then gradually open the distances out.

'We invariably approach all grids from trot, so the first elements are nearly always a placing pole to a cross-pole, followed by whatever you want to practise, for example a double bounce, one stride to a bounce, and so on.

'You can devise any number of combinations in a grid, but the objective should always be to improve the horse's technique and to prepare him for what he may meet in competition. It is important to keep that aim in view, or you can easily dishearten a horse.'

GRIDWORK FOR THE VERY NOVICE HORSE

'In the first sequence of pictures this horse's inexperience is evident in the way he is looking at the poles, and dangling his legs over the cross-pole; his mind is on the line of poles on the floor and he is not really thinking about the fence. This shows clearly the other reason for working a young horse through grids: getting him used to seeing a line of obstacles in front of him so he learns to take it all in his stride.

'The next time the horse approaches the grid looking far more confident and organised. The grid is gradually made more demanding, first by putting in a small upright one stride from the cross-pole, then by adding a parallel two strides from the upright. In both cases we leave the canter poles in place to help the horse lighten his forehand as he progresses through the grid.

Leslie schools a young or an inexperienced horse over grids twice a week, the aim being to make the horse more athletic and to encourage him to use himself properly and jump in a correct style. Gridwork forms a good foundation for all jump training, as by making the horse more athletic it will inevitably be easier for him to jump in a correct style, which is to lower his head and neck, to elevate his shoulders, and to snap up his front legs. It also introduces him to the idea of combination fences.

'We start off all the novice horses with the following warm-up exercise: trot to a placing pole, set at about 8 feet from a small cross-pole; this is followed by a series of canter poles, the first set 9 feet from the cross-pole on the landing side, followed by five or six more set at 9 to 10 feet,' explains Leslie. 'As the young horse lands over the fence, the canter poles help keep his stride elevated by picking him up off his forehand after he has

jumped. This sort of exercise also gets him used to seeing a line of poles set out in front of him, and having to find his feet through them – at a later date this could be a series of obstacles. All the rider should do is bring the horse into the grid in a steady, balanced trot. Everything is set up for the horse, so the rider can concentrate on keeping a strong lower leg with the weight down in the heel, and keeping the upper body in balance with the horse. *Let* the horse make his mistakes at this level so that he learns from them; simply adjust the poles and the distances to suit his stride and to help improve his technique.

On the following pages Harriet rides the six-year-old Odin, by Cruise Missile, which has been sent to Leslie to produce as an event horse. He is out of a Grade B showjumper and so has all the right credentials, but he still has a great deal to learn.

'Odin has a tendency to drift to the right over his fences, and this is something we would hope to correct as soon as possible. It is important that the horse is taught to jump straight: firstly it enables him to push off the ground with equal strength in both hindquarters, therefore allowing him to throw a more powerful jump; and secondly it is now essential on today's cross-country courses to be able to ride a straight, accurate line through combinations.

◀ 'Rather than have the rider interfering with the horse's balance by trying to haul him back on line, we use guiding poles to encourage him to jump straight, so that he learns *himself* to keep true to a line. This sequence of pictures shows how using poles prevents Odin from drifting to the right, and encourages him to "think straight" himself. The rider can also open the rein to draw the horse away from the side he likes to drift, and it is important that he does react to any non-straightness in this way so he can straighten the horse up should he drift at a competition where there won't be any poles to help him. But at home, using poles makes the horse correct himself and is hopefully a more meaningful lesson to him than letting him always rely on the rider to keep him on course.

'The grid can be further developed until it consists of the placing pole to the cross-pole, followed by two oxers set two strides apart, with canter poles in between. Odin still has quite a lot to learn and he is not neat enough with his front legs yet, but the double of oxers will help teach him this. He is still looking at everything that is put in front of him, which will be an asset later on in life as long as he maintains his forward momentum while he is looking. We finish off by cantering him to an upright fence with V poles, an arrangement which

▼

again encourages the horse to snap up his front legs; the photo shows how he is beginning to make better use of himself.

▼

'Once a horse is jumping comfortably through this type of grid and has got used to jumping in a correct style, I would then introduce bounces. The canter poles already used in the grid do actually form "little bounces", and so it shouldn't be too difficult a progression to go from these to bouncing over small fences. Use a single bounce first, always ensuring that the second element of the bounce is slightly higher than the first so that the horse can see exactly what is required as he comes into it. Once he has got the idea you can go to a double bounce, and then begin to incorporate these into more complex grids.'

FURTHER GRIDWORK

The grey horse featured in the picture sequences is 'Smiley', a novice horse which Leslie had been asked to sell. He starts off with the usual warm-up exercises: a placing pole to a cross-pole followed by canter poles. An upright is then added, using planks, set one stride from the cross-pole, leaving a canter pole between the two jumps, and then three or four after the planks.

'This grid has clearly helped the horse to make a really nice shape over the planks; he has come in, lowered his head and neck and used himself well. Harriet has stayed in balance with him and is concentrating on keeping a strong lower leg and on keeping him straight; as we have already said, even that is something which can be aided by using poles, leaving the rider to concentrate solely on leg and body position.

'To complete the schooling session for this horse we added a parallel one stride from the planks, again leaving the canter poles in position: note that a square parallel generally helps teach the horse to be sharper with his front legs; whereas the ascending parallel encourages the horse to let go behind so that he flicks his hindlegs over the fences and doesn't drag them through it. In this particular picture the horse has really snapped up his front legs, clearly showing that the square parallel he jumped just before this did its job well.'

4 Cross-Country Schooling

'The purpose of cross-country schooling is to teach horse and rider how to deal with the type of things that they will meet on the cross-country course at a competition. It doesn't matter if the competition fences are bigger or more substantial than those you have schooled over, as long as you have both seen, and tackled, similar questions when schooling. Horses are very similar to children in that some can handle new challenges better than others simply because they are more talented or naturally gifted in that direction. Cross-country schooling is like preparing a child for an exam; no one knows what the actual questions on the day will be, but if they have been given a good general grounding then they should have sufficient knowledge to expand upon, and tackle whatever arises on the day. So for the horse, his jump schooling at home is his basic "classwork" and the competition cross-country course is the exam. You will find that some horses, like people, work better under exam pressure, whereas others will work well at home but will not perform so well at an event.

'So the aim when schooling is to practise over fences which resemble the type of thing you will meet at an event. The fences you practise over should not be so big as to frighten horse or rider, but whatever you jump you must insist on obedience in the approach, on straightness and accuracy. For example, if you set up a narrow corner using showjump poles at home, jump it right on the point of the corner so that you test your ability to ride a line, and your horse's ability to stay on that line.

'I never school across country over anything higher than 3ft 6in, and with my Pre-Novice horses I wouldn't jump anything even that high before their first event. If they have got the scope they will always jump the bigger fences as long as they are confident about what they are doing, so at home you want it to be a pleasure for them.

'A great deal can be achieved at home by imaginative use of showjump poles and other equipment; we usually introduce the young horses to coffins, corners and arrowheads at home using showjump poles and barrels, jump fillers and suchlike. It is very unlikely that I would take a young horse to a proper cross-country schooling course more than four times before he does his first event, and with the more experienced horses I might school them somewhere just once before the start of the competition season. With an Advanced horse like Haig I wouldn't bother to school across country at all, although a less experienced horse like Sidney's King, for example, I would pop over a few Novice fences before his first event, just to settle him down and to give him a chance to "get his eye in". After that I would only school the more experienced horses if they were having problems with a particular type of fence.

'When a new horse comes into the yard I will nearly always school that once, just to get a feel of how it reacts to things, but when I am offered a chance ride at an event I usually know the horse from having seen him on the competition circuit and have a good idea of what he is like – and I can usually get some tips from the last jockey!

'Someone with only one or two horses to ride may want to school more than this to get as much practice and experience as possible. I am competing every weekend, often on four or five horses, as well as riding just as many at least every day at home, and so obviously I do get a lot more practice than the rider with only one or two.

'I do believe that the young horse needs assistance on the approach to his fences, so that he comes to them in a balanced way and meets the fence on a good stride. Some riders believe, and teach, that you should just let the horse run down to the fence and sort himself out, but I consider that to do this causes the horse to lose confidence, and that it is a technique which will run him into trouble as the fences get bigger and more technical. The best riders today are able to help their horses on the approach to a fence, this optimises their chance of jumping well and safely, and ultimately produces a top class, confident horse – and that is what we are all striving for.

'For cross-country and showjumping it is

important to teach the young horse to lighten his front end as he comes to a fence, and to hold himself off it. In the long term, if a horse has always been disciplined to do this, his rider will then find it easy to ride him forwards up to his fences, with his hindquarters engaged. This is the approach I like to make to almost every type of fence: I lighten the front end, and then ride the horse forwards up to the base of the fence, with his forehand elevated and his hindquarters engaged. When Haig and Chessman, both Advanced horses, sight a fence now I can feel them automatically bringing up their front end as they approach it, making their frame shorter and more collected and "sitting down on their hindquarters" – in this type of balance the rider can then be quite confident about being able to ride forwards to the fence safely, with the horse off his forehand.

'A young horse will tend to fall on his forehand, especially if he is ridden forwards to the fence without first having been taught to lighten his front end. It is important that he learns to allow his rider to ride him up to the base of a fence, and to be light in front. If he is always allowed to go on a long stride and to stand off his fences he will learn to drag his rider into each one; he will be on his forehand, and will not be able to use himself properly, and once the fences get bigger and more technical he really will have problems because he will always try to quicken to his fences and will flatten out over them, making it harder for himself to jump them cleanly. However, if he is ridden up to the base of the fence he has to elevate his front end, snap up

his front legs neatly, and jump in a good shape.

'If I am riding a horse which does drag me into a fence and which won't listen when I ask it to wait, then I use the rein contact to "bump" it off its stride: normally when in canter, you allow your hands to move forwards with each stride, following the contact. However, if I need to make a horse wait and listen to me on the approach to a fence, instead of following the contact I will take a firm pull, then quickly release the contact again, and this is generally sufficient to knock the horse out of the stride that he was set on. Now, either he has to sort himself out in a bit of a hurry as things are no longer going as he planned, or he has to wait for me to tell him what to do. The latter is what I am aiming for, and so until he does learn to listen I either do this, or perhaps circle him away from the fence if there is room to do so. The aim of each exercise is the same – to make the horse wait for, and listen to, his rider.

'It is interesting to watch a video of the 1994 Grand National, and to see how Dunwoody's horse, Minnehoma, elevated his front end each time his jockey pushed him up to a fence; this meant he was in good balance both on the approach and on landing after each one. Double Silk, on the other hand, who looked to be jumping for fun, proved too scopey for his own good. He was galloping and jumping beautifully out of his stride, but was standing off further and further until finally he overstretched himself, by which time he had run himself too much onto his forehand to be able to save himself from falling.'

Seeing Your Distance

Much of Leslie's own jump training took place in America, when he spent two years with Ian Silitch. There, great emphasis was placed on teaching riders to help the horse reach a consistently good take-off point at its fences. Some riders have a natural eye for this, and as they come to a fence they don't even have to think about the adjustment they need to make in order to meet it on a good distance. A good many, however, have to teach themselves this art, and Leslie feels very strongly that riders *should* make the effort to learn this skill if it does not come naturally to them. 'There are people who will tell you just to kick on and let the horse sort himself out,' says Leslie, 'but unless you have an exceptionally bold and talented horse you will either end up wrecking his confidence, or running him into trouble once he moves out of Novice classes and has to tackle the bigger and more technical fences.

'One way of helping riders to create rhythm and balance, and the ability to see a distance to a fence, is to set up lines of fences at different related distances. For example, put up a small fence, just a cross-pole if you like, and then build a small spread fence at an exact distance away – say, five strides. The rider should be able to canter to this and ride five even strides from the first jump to the next: this exercise therefore gives him a feel for the pace, rhythm and balance needed to fit in the correct number of strides. If he over-rides then he will fit in fewer strides, and if he checks the horse too much he will fit in too many; and so this simple exercise may also help in diagnosing what a rider may have been doing wrong if he has been having trouble with his jumping. Ridden correctly, this exercise also means that, because the distance between the two fences is fixed, the horse will always reach the second fence

at the same point of take-off; so it enables the rider to see and feel what that distance is, and gradually to train himself always to try and ride to it. That is to say, once his eye has adjusted to this particular distance, he should start to get a feel for the length of stride required, and the rhythm and the balance needed to meet the fence at a comfortable take-off point every time. The more this is practised, the easier it should become to start seeing and feeling the stride needed when riding to a single fence. This sort of exercise is unlimited, and the distance can be opened out to as many strides as you want: a line of fences can be set up on short or long distances so that the rider gets a feel for what he must do to adjust to them. Every rider should "play" with distances at home, in the same way that the course designer will play with them to test competitors at an event.

▲

In the photographs Leslie is schooling a five-year-old, Blue Laser, for the very first time. 'This is the sort of approach I am talking about; the horse's natural reaction as he canters to the little log is to start to look up to see what it is. I support him with the lower leg, and by not chasing him into the fence, his front end automatically comes up as he approaches this strange object. On the last stride I just allow my arms to stretch forwards a little as he lowers his head and neck slightly to look at the fence, then he just pops over it in the style I am looking for.

'This fence is only about a foot high, so obviously the horse is quite able to jump it with very little pace – even if he stopped in front of it, he could be pushed over it. By starting off over such small jumps horse and rider are much more likely to stay relaxed, and there is less risk of the rider panicking and starting to chase the horse into the fence. Usually I let a horse jump quietly backwards and forwards over each fence until he feels happy and comfortable with it, and then we move on to the next fence.

▲

'A few hundred yards from the first little log was a tiger trap. In this sort of situation I would let the horse jump the log, and then canter up to and round the tiger trap before turning back to jump the log again. Then the next time we jumped the log I would just keep him cantering quietly up to the tiger trap, and over he would go!

'I chose the next few fences because they were alongside a wall, so the horse was held in on one side; like this, the rider only has to worry about making sure that it doesn't run out to the right. So here I concentrate on riding the horse forwards and keeping his neck very slightly flexed to the right so that he can't bulge out through his right shoulder. I hold him between hand and leg all the way to the fence, and on the last stride I just allow him to lower his head and neck to the fence as he goes to take off. Any horse is bigger and stronger than its rider, so if it is really determined to run out or stop, then it will; but a lot of problems can be avoided by the rider being prepared for this sort of thing and reacting accordingly. So with this young horse we have only jumped small fences; they can be jumped out of a steady canter, and at this pace it is easier to balance him and be in control of what is happening. They are small enough to pop from a standstill if he did decide to stop, and here we have also made use of the wall when introducing him to fences which are new to him, to help us keep him straight.

'At this stage in a horse's training, and when jumping fences this size and at this pace, I would expect him to take off about 1–2 yards from the base of the fence. However, I do not look at this "take-off point" as I approach the fence, because the last place a rider should be looking is down; I focus on the top rail of the fence I am jumping as this helps to keep my head and my eyesight up, and this in turn helps keep the horse's front end up; and I also find that doing this brings me in to the take-off point I want. This sort of approach keeps everything simple and unhurried for the horse; standing off a fence requires much more effort, and simply encourages a horse to fall on his forehand. At a later stage you will find that your take-off distance varies according to the type of fence. For example if I am galloping to a hedge or a nice ascending spread, I may let the horse take off up to three yards from the fence. But before a rider can do this, he has to know that he can then bring the horse back if necessary and get him really short and collected for the next fence which, if it is a bounce or a coffin, requires a powerful bouncy stride on the approach, and a much more controlled and contained style of jumping.

COFFIN FENCES

'Before I ask a young horse to jump a proper cross-country coffin, I would always school it at home first, over one made up with showjumps. When a horse is first asked to jump a coffin his eye is usually on the ditch in the middle, and sometimes he just forgets to take off over the rail coming in. So it is safer for all concerned if that rail can fall down; no one gets hurt, and just as importantly, no one's confidence is harmed, either.

'Generally we put up a small showjump as the first element, and then use either a water tray or feed sacks held down with poles to simulate a ditch. Another showjump can be added to form the final element. The horse should be allowed to pop the "ditch" first, and then jump the ditch to the rail; then turn him round and jump the rail to the ditch, and finally include the rail out. Once a horse is quite happy with this sort of combination it is a good idea to "play" with the distances, so that eventually he might bounce from the rail to the ditch to the rail.

'The first priority is always to get the horse through this sort of combination without stopping. If he does stop, say at the jump going in, then he must be held there and not allowed to turn away while someone lowers the fence so that he can step over it. The first objective of the exercise is to hold him straight and insist that he goes forwards, even if the pole is on the ground; only then can the fence be gradually built back up, until he tackles it properly. At a proper cross-country course it is still very important to introduce a coffin combination in stages, by jumping the ditch in the middle first, then including one rail at a time, before attempting it as a true combination.

'The approach to a coffin should always be more collected than to a straightforward fence – it is much more like a showjumping canter, with not too much pace but plenty of controlled power or impulsion. The horse must be given time to see where he is going, and he needs to jump in neatly so that he is sufficiently balanced and organised to jump the ditch and the exit rail. The rider should keep the lower leg very firmly in position, and controls the pace by sitting with the shoulders elevated and by keeping a firm contact, so that he contains and directs the power that is being created by his lower leg. Then if the horse decides it doesn't like the look of where it has to go, he will nevertheless be 'holding' enough stored-up energy to still send it forwards with sufficient momentum to jump what is in front of it. The main thing is confidence; once the rider is confident about the pace and balance needed to tackle this sort of fence, and the horse knows what a coffin entails, then both horse and rider should be prepared to tackle any coffin-type combination.

'It is tempting to draw a comparison with

confident children – they may be obnoxious with it – but they always seem to get on in life! One of our best Novice horses, George, is a quite obnoxious creature to deal with, but he will also be a great horse as he is supremely confident. But then he should be, as so far he has had a wonderful "upbringing": he has seen nothing in life to frighten him as yet, and if we continue to produce him carefully, there is no reason why anything should ever frighten or worry him.

'However, we can all still get caught out! Those who compete at Badminton and have to tackle the coffin there will find how easily it can be misjudged – but then, that is all part of the uniqueness and unpredictability of the big three-day events.

'In this picture sequence another young horse, Dan Dare, is being asked to jump a trakehner for the first time. The fence is only about two feet high and once again, by having a steady approach and keeping the horse between hand and leg it should still be possible to hold him to the fence and persuade him to pop over it, whatever he tries to do. Dan is quite shocked by the trakehner, but I have kept the leg on and said, "Come on, just get on with it!" and he does that for me. However, as can be seen in the second picture, I really needed to have been sitting in behind the horse more, as his hesitation has tipped me forwards and my weight is now loading his shoulders – he could quite easily have put his front feet back down at this point and stopped. After this we just canter backwards and forwards over the fence until he is confident.

'Had we been schooling over a bigger fence he might well have decided to stop the first time, and this is something every trainer should try to avoid at all costs: it is not good policy for the young horse to discover that he can stop if he feels like it; it is essential to convince him that he has to keep going forwards, always, no matter what he is faced with. A trakehner is a trakehner, and once he knows what it is he shouldn't be worried about jumping a bigger version of the same sort of fence at an event. As always, it is the appearance of the fence, rather than the size of it, which the trainer must school the horse to accept. Size is really only a problem if the horse lacks scope, in which case it would be wrong to persevere with him over cross-country courses that are patently too big for his ability; you would have to be content with competing only at a level he can cope with.

'A trakehner-type fence can also be practised at home, by putting a showjump across your "coffin ditch". Simulating cross-country fences in this way means you can practise a lot of things at home without spending time and money on trips to schooling courses.'

INTRODUCING WATER

'When introducing a horse to water the most important thing is to choose a complex where he can walk in the first time. When hacking out, we always encourage the horse to walk through puddles, in the hope that they will not find it too much of a shock when they are asked to walk into an extra big puddle. The golden rule is to keep it simple. I always leave the water fence until near the end of the schooling session. The horse will already have jumped ditches, steps, banks and so on, and having done a fair bit of work, should be more amenable by this stage. Besides, should the worst happen and I get soaked through at least there is no more schooling still to do!

'So generally I just walk the horse in and let him wander around and get used to it – he can paw it, drink it, sniff it, whatever he wants, so that he realises it is harmless. Generally, a horse will walk in quite happily – though some might stop several strides away, or right on the edge. It is important not to hassle him too much at this early stage; keep him faced up to the water, but give him time to weigh up the situation. You may need to use your stick to send him in eventually, or even someone on the ground with a lunge whip. Either way it is important to be prepared for this, and have someone there to help if the horse is determined not to go in. As long as you are fair and clear about what you want, then no harm can be done by resorting to these methods. But give the horse a chance first; if he says "No", then first use more leg; if he still argues, give him a couple of slaps with the stick as well; and if he is still not persuaded, only then use outside help with a lunge whip and lunge line if necessary. It is important that the rider doesn't lose this battle. However, using this approach I have never had much difficulty introducing a horse to water – a couple of slaps with the stick are usually enough – unless the horse has come to me with a specific problem with water.

'It is always advisable to take someone with you when you go for a cross-country school, just in case anything goes wrong; and if you take a lunge whip, then he or she can back you up if necessary. It is very seldom that the horse will ever need touching with the whip; it is usually enough for him to realise that there is another driving force besides the rider. However, if a horse is very difficult then it is important that the rider can keep both hands on the reins and can concentrate on keeping the horse straight, whilst his aids are backed up by someone behind with a lunge whip. In the case of introducing him to water, once he goes in, don't let

him shoot straight out the other side but make him stay in it until he is settled and relaxed. A young horse in particular needs a chance to acclimatise to this new situation – much of his fear is instinctive – and he must be shown that there is nothing to fear. Once he is walking in and out of the water quite happily, ask him to trot through.

'The next stage is to trot in over a small log, or to

drop down into the water (see photos). On the approach it is essential to have enough pace and determination so that the horse knows he has to go, but without hassling or driving him too hard. As he jumps in, lean back and slip the reins, though still keep the contact. Once in the water contact must be maintained, and the horse kept between hand and leg; hold him together as he crosses the water to meet the step out. Don't be in a hurry to push him up the step, and make sure you don't tip the upper body forwards to meet the step. The drag of the water always makes it harder for the horse to lift his front end, and so the rider must keep his or her weight back behind the movement; this means he is then in a safer position if the horse trips or misses the step, and it gives the horse the freedom to lift his front end clear of the step out.

'By the end of the schooling session I would expect the horse to be cantering in and out of the water confidently, when the same principles apply: keep the contact, keep the weight back behind the horse and don't rush him.'

STRAIGHTNESS AND ACCURACY

▲

'In any jump schooling session it is very important that the horse stays straight. It may not seem vital at the time, but in the long term, on today's cross-country courses, straightness and accuracy constantly come into play.

'Straightening poles and using an "open hand" have already been discussed, and in the picture sequence Odin is being "straightened out" with an open hand in a practice session at home. Using an "open hand" can upset the jump that the horse then produces as it may cause him to hollow, but it is more important to instil straightness into the horse at this juncture than to worry about protecting the jump. If no effort is made to sort these problems out at home they will only get worse under the pressure of an event. Very few horses are one hundred per cent straight through their bodies, and most favour one side or the other. Quite often the horse's strong or weak side correlates to the rider's; for example Harriet, who does much of the flatwork schooling, finds that the horses get stronger in the left rein after I have ridden them, because I am left-handed and so take a stronger hold of that rein without even realising it. So she then works on softening the horse to the left so that this one-sidedness doesn't become a problem.

'The arrowhead fence is a popular inclusion in many courses nowadays, and we spend a lot of time practising over narrow obstacles at home because of this. We use either barrels or showjump fillers – ours are only six feet wide so they are ideal for this purpose. By practising over this type of fence at home, however, you would hope to have instilled in the horse the conviction that the fence is there to be jumped, and then you would feel confident either to ride him up to it on a longer stride so that he made up the distance, or to sit in behind him and let him pop in another stride.

'In the picture sequence above we introduce George to an arrowhead fence for the first time; to make it easier for him to understand what we want, we have put guide poles which act as wings facing towards him. He has immediately focussed on the fence and doesn't worry about jumping it at all.

'We then build it up until we have a combination of this first arrowhead, followed by two strides to a showjump gate, then four strides to another arrowhead, but this time with the arms facing away from us. As George lands over the gate he does focus on the arrowhead but he is just starting to look a bit confused, and runs out. It would be wrong to get cross with him, he just needs time to work out what is required. So we turn back and jump through the sequence again, this time successfully.

'If he had run out a second time, then we would have put the guide poles round the other way so that they helped to guide him in. Once a horse understands what is expected of him, then the poles can be put back the other way and you can try again.'

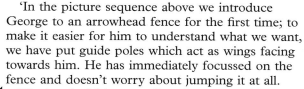

5 Cross-Country Course Design

One of the greatest attractions of BHS eventing, as opposed to unaffiliated competitions, is the consistently high standard of its cross-country courses.

Although eventing as a sport is designed to test the riders' skill in all three phases – the dressage, showjumping and cross-country – it is generally the cross-country which makes the strongest impression on both the riders and spectators.

APPROVING A COURSE

Before a new event is given the go-ahead, both the site and the organiser have to be approved, usually by the HTG regional director and sometimes also by the technical adviser. These will want to know who is to design the course, as that person is then expected to liaise with the technical adviser throughout its planning. The technical adviser's input will vary from virtually designing the course himself, to simply approving the plans put in front of him; whichever is the case, visits will be made to the site while the course is being built so that any suggested alterations can be made before construction is too far advanced. Finally the finished course must be approved by the BHS steward the day before the event. In the case of a new event the BHS steward and the technical adviser would inspect the near-completed course well before the event date.

TECHNICAL ADVISERS

The Horse Trials Group employs about nine technical advisers who are paid on a daily basis, the amount depending upon how many courses each is responsible for. The HTG is always looking out for potential trainees, although it must also ensure that those who are already trained have got enough work to do. People interested in becoming technical advisers usually approach the HTG personally to express their interest; they then become trainees for six to twelve months, travelling round various events with a qualified TA. To succeed they need some knowledge and experience, and a good deal of tact, diplomacy and firmness.

New events are usually allocated the more experienced TAs, and new TAs are usually put in charge of the more established events to begin with. Some people remain working at Novice level while others progress right through the ranks to work at international championships.

BHS STEWARDS

BHS stewards are volunteers; they are not expected to be experts on the cross-country phase, though in fact they are often ex-competitors or event organisers. They are normally expected to take the technical adviser's advice on matters relating to the cross-country, but they do have the right not to do so. However, the general principle is that if a steward disagrees about a fence, then the solution should err towards adopting the easier option rather than the more difficult.

Having passed the cross-country course as suitable, at the event itself the BHS steward is in charge of resolving all arguments and objections. The technical adviser usually attends the event and acts as assistant steward, and it would be his responsibility to brief the fence judges.

CONCEPTION AND DESIGN
by Mike Etherington-Smith

Mike Etherington-Smith is the course designer and director of Blenheim CCI***, and competed as an event rider himself before he became increasingly involved in course design. When he gave up riding he turned his attention to this work full time and now designs courses all over the world.

'A great many people like to have a go at designing cross-country courses, but there is a lot more to it than most of us imagine. The result is a wide variety in standards of course design around the world, not just in the UK. It is essential to spend time playing with ideas, watching, assessing and experimenting. It simply doesn't work just to build a number of fences and to call it a course, because all you have is a series of obstacles: in a proper course there is a relationship between them, and every fence is there for a reason.

'A course must have flow and feel – having been an event rider myself proved to be a useful asset as hopefully it has given me a feel for what horses can and can't do, and for what is a fair or an unfair question. Riding bad horses in particular gives you an understanding of what is fair or otherwise! Any would-be course designer should spend time at events just watching how horses cover the ground, and how they jump different types of fences off different terrain; he should look to see which fences don't seem to ride well and note why, so that he doesn't repeat the same mistake on his own course.

'Whilst having ridden has been helpful to me I am not sure that it is a pre-requisite of being a good course designer. However, it *is* important to understand what a horse can do on different types of terrain, and also to appreciate the ability of the riders at any particular level – one of the hardest things is to get the standard right for the level you are designing for. There can be no compromise on this: a designer must have a standard in mind and then build up to that standard, and those riders who are not good enough will simply not get round. However, he also has a responsibility to the horses, and must ensure that they do not suffer because their riders lack ability. All this must be taken into account when designing a course and the overriding priority for every designer is safety.

'The standard of every course is geared to the three-day events at international level, that is the CCI one-, two-, three- and four-star events. Because the one-day events are used as qualifications for these big three-day events, their standard is based on the degree of ability that horse and rider will be expected to show at the CCIs. So the Novice, Intermediate and Advanced one-day events are largely responsible for preparing horse and rider for the courses they will have to tackle at each three-day event of the appropriate level.'

DESIGNING A NEW COURSE

'When a designer is asked to build a new course he must have a very clear idea of the standard he is designing for, and the rules that appertain to that level of competition. He also needs to know the objectives in mind for the particular event: where it "fits" in the seasonal calendar, if the organiser wants an encouraging, first-timers' course or something more testing, and so on.

'There are a huge number of variables to consider when designing a course in a new venue: access, car parking, the convenience factor for the public and the competitors, and at the bigger events, considerations have to be made for TV cameras and suchlike. Personally when I design a course my priorities are first, the horse, and then the public, and everything else has to fit around these two things. After that I spend a lot of time studying the site, getting a feel for the place, and weighing up various alternatives. I need to know what the budget is, or at least the upper limit, as this obviously has a tremendous effect on what you can or cannot do. The budget has to cover my fee, the course builders' fee and the cost of materials.

Choosing the start and finish points

'One of the first things to establish about the course is where the start and finish can be; in particular, at one-day events, this should be relevant to the lorry park, but it must also be found and reached easily by the public, and situated sensibly from a safety point of view. A flat or an uphill finish is better than a situation where a galloping horse has to be pulled up while running downhill.

Planning the route

'From this point the designer then finds his route or track. Beware, because if there are a lot of natural features then it is easy to overdo it. What he should be looking for is a horse-friendly route – that is, if someone set off from the start for a canter, would he be able to follow the route without having to haul his horse around? After that, most courses virtually design themselves due to the area and the terrain available. The course should flow: the first part should encourage the horse to run and jump out of a rhythm, then the questions should be introduced towards the middle. You are lucky if there is more than one possible site for a water complex, and once this is established fences can be designed that incorporate, where possible, the natural features of the land.

'I like to get horses jumping really well early on the course. The maximum Novice height of 3ft 6in is well within the scope of most horses, but within these parameters I try to design the first few fences so that they do get the horse off the ground and encourage him to use his scope. Then I start to introduce the questions, although at whatever level the course is designed for, after setting a difficult fence I then slip in one which will restore confidence if needs be.

'At Novice level the emphasis should be on educating rather than on continually trying to test horse and rider; as you progress up the scale the balance between educating and testing alters, so that at Badminton, for example, the aim is more to test rather than to try to educate. It is also important to remember that there is no such thing as the ultimate event; there is always another one at which the rider will wish to compete, so I want a horse to be learning as he goes round a course, and to finish well and happy. I want the rider to learn more about his horse as he goes round the track, and to discover his own ability, or lack of it. These days there is more emphasis on the rider's ability and his understanding of the relationship between fences; so if *he* makes a mistake, it is essential that the horse is not punished as a result whenever possible. Riders often seem to think there is a "them and us" situation between course designers and competitors, and feel that the designer is trying to catch them out. However, they must remember that it is a competition, and that the aim of the course designer should be to test how well prepared the horse and rider are. A few years ago there were certain incidents when riders were rightly aggrieved as some designers were beginning to set up fences that caught out the horse rather than the rider.

Problem fences

'It should be quite feasible to design courses that test the rider, but without punishing the horse if his rider

is not up to scratch. The arrowhead fence and angled combinations, for example, are now commonly used, and although riders tend not to like them it really should not be that difficult to ride a horse on a straight line to a narrow target area. It is a basic skill that all riders need to be able to achieve, for safety's sake – for example, when jumping a corner it is essential to hold a line and aim at a relatively narrow, jumpable section of the fence; and if a rider can't do this he will either have a run-out or, worse, land his horse in the middle of the section that is too wide to jump. An arrowhead fence asks exactly the same question of the rider but is even kinder to the horse, because should he duck out, he will not be running himself into trouble whichever side he veers off.

Fences on a turn

'Putting two fences around a turn is another question I like to ask, when essentially I am testing the rider's ability either to hold a straight line and jump at an angle over both fences, or to land, turn, and still ride smoothly forwards to the second element. If the rider does not have this ability, hopefully the worst that could happen to the horse is that he will stop or run out.

Related distances

'With the same intention the designer might leave a related distance of, say, four or five strides between two fences – particularly useful on a downhill slope,

this provides ample opportunity for riders to mess things up, because even though the distance is set up for them, very few can resist either taking a pull somewhere between the two, or driving the horse on, or sometimes both! Either way it is easy to mess up the distance that has been given to them. What the course designer hopes is that gradually the rider will learn to stop interfering with the horse, beyond keeping him balanced and straight, and to leave him just to run and jump out of his stride in this sort of situation.

'It is important to introduce riders to these sorts of questions as soon as they come into the sport. If they learn how to tackle all these things when the fences are only small at Novice, or even Pre-Novice level, then they will be well prepared should they upgrade to Intermediate and Advanced. This is something that perhaps isn't done enough. I certainly think that as far as Pre-Novice is concerned, the right standard has not yet been set for the courses. Any horse should be able to jump 3ft 6in and so the fences should not necessarily be smaller than at Novice level – the course should still prepare horse and rider for what the cross-country phase of the sport of eventing is all about. Too many of the courses are so easy that riders just chase their horses round, not needing either to train or to prepare them to a particularly high standard at home; the poor horse then arrives at a Novice event and neither he nor his rider are properly prepared for what faces them. It is this sort of situation that sees a lowering in the standard of competition riding.'

6 Practical Cross-Country Riding

The rider will prepare himself and his horse as well as possible at home, but the real test comes in actual competition.

The following pages cover a variety of events, from Pre-Novice through to the Badminton three-day event. The 1994 season did not run as smoothly as Leslie would have hoped. He broke his ankle as the result of a fall at Dynes Hall Advanced, and so was unable to ride at Badminton. He suffered a second accident in the summer when a novice horse ran into a tree with him at Stowe one-day event. The subsequent concussion and damaged shoulder healed sufficiently for him to ride Haig at Gatcombe, but then Haig went lame the week before his autumn target of Burghley three-day event, and he had to be withdrawn.

However, all this is very much what the sport of eventing is all about: coping with the highs and lows. Leslie was greatly encouraged by the progress of his younger rides throughout the season, and he describes, where appropriate, how he tackled each event, at the different levels, with each of them.

EARLY PLANS FOR THE YOUNG EVENT HORSE

'Ideally I like to be able to start training a potential event horse during the winter prior to the start of his first event season. Once I feel his work is established nicely on the flat, and that he is jumping confidently through grids and round small courses at home, I would start to compete with him indoors at both dressage and showjumping competitions. By the start of the event season I would like him to be jumping clear round Discovery and Newcomers courses; besides this, if his temperament allowed it, I would give him three or four days' hunting, and then he would have two or three cross-country schooling sessions. The idea behind all this is to get him out and about and experiencing all sorts of different things, but without putting too much pressure on him.

'When starting the season with a five-year-old, I would probably aim to do two or three Pre-Novice events with him before asking him to tackle one at Novice level – there is no need to rush things with a horse of this age, and it is better to establish plenty of confidence in him before asking any harder questions. On the other hand, if I had a seven-year-old which had not evented before but which had been to a few competitions and had perhaps hunted, then I would do just one Pre-Novice before trying a Novice class, if all had gone well.

'I will always keep a horse in Novice classes until I feel confident that he is ready to upgrade to Intermediate; for some horses this might be after six events, for others it could be after a dozen, or maybe never – there are very many horses that never make it to Intermediate level. Usually the horse tells you, by the feel he gives you, whether or not he is ready to upgrade. A horse that has learned how to gallop and has got plenty of scope would only need holding back if he were very young. The seven-year-old, for example, I would just allow to progress naturally. A lot depends also on whether you are hoping to qualify for a three-day event; if so, it is important to take into account the time needed to fit in all the rounds necessary to qualify: for example, if the aim is to do a spring CCI★★ then you really need to start tackling Intermediate courses the season before. The present rules [1994] stipulate that five clear rounds at Intermediate level are required in order to do a two-star event, and that is plenty enough to accomplish in the early part of a new season.

'I would try to keep a six-year-old horse at Novice level for longer if possible, as probably I would not want to do a two-star event with him until the end of his seventh year. There are exceptions, however – George is only five but he has done two Novice events already this year,

and I might consider doing a two-star event with him at the end of his sixth year – but then he is a particularly talented and bold horse. As I said, the horse will usually tell you what he is ready to do.

'When it comes to upgrading to Advanced, it is probably harder to find what is, to my mind, a true first-time Advanced course; in fact most Advanced tracks just seem to get harder and harder each year. Nevertheless, once the horse is finding Intermediate courses well within his scope and ability – that is, he is not looking into deep ditches, hesitating in front of water, or leaving a leg behind on the way into combinations such as coffins – then it is fair enough to try him at Advanced level. I would want him to have jumped his last three or four Intermediates really well in order to feel sufficiently confident about upgrading him. On the other hand, if a horse keeps picking up points but is still a bit green about things, then keep competing him at Open or Advanced Intermediate level; don't attempt an Advanced cross-country course until you both feel really confident.

'At Advanced level, if I find myself riding a horse that does not feel confident or happy on the course, then I would not be afraid to pull him up and retire. I would always give him a chance to "find his feet" over the first five or six fences, but if he doesn't open up and take the course on a bit after that, then I would stop him. I would take him back to Intermediate level and wait for some improvement before trying an Advanced track again. Furthermore, always bear in mind that some horses will never be capable of upgrading. And if you don't have much experience yourself and are not sure whether it is you or the horse that is struggling at this level, then it is well worth asking a more experienced rider to take him round a course, to assess him for you. If he is willing to ride him again the chances are you have got a good horse!'

Longleat provides very fair Pre-Novice and Novice courses but when Leslie went, heavy rain during the previous week had made the ground conditions testing. The terrain is reasonably demanding at the best of times, with its undulations, but combined with the heavy going many horses were making hard work of it; on the Novice track there were some fairly stiff combinations towards the end of the course which were tiring for the horses in these conditions. Leslie rode George and Cruiseway in the Pre-Novice, but he withdrew all his Novice horses on the day as the ground conditions deteriorated. For George it was his third Pre-Novice, and it was the first event of this season for Cruiseway. George had been scheduled to do a Novice after Aldon, which was his second Pre-Novice outing, but because of the long break when Leslie fractured his ankle it was thought wiser to do another Pre-Novice before upgrading him.

'The ascending palisade at fence 4 was a very inviting fence in itself, but it was sited downhill and had quite a significant drop on it for a Pre-Novice. As you came to the brow of the hill on the approach it was important to balance the horse and get him light in front – you can't afford to let a young horse run downhill on his forehand and be heavy on your hand, even to a kind fence like this one. Concentrate on keeping the horse balanced all the way to the fence, with the upper body more elevated than usual – the shoulders could even be back a touch – and with the weight well down in the heel. On reaching the fence, release with the arms to give the horse the freedom to use himself over it, but maintain the contact throughout to support and balance him.

'In the photos you can see that Lucinda Murray has the horse light in front with his hindquarters driven well underneath him. She has followed his movement with the hand, and has maintained the contact throughout without restricting him at all; on landing, she has closed her lower leg and held the contact to help him pick himself up after the drop. In heavy ground it is even more important to be in balance on landing so that you can help, rather than hinder the horse as he tries to lift himself out of the mud.

'Another challenge on the Pre-Novice course was the post-and-rail drop, followed a few strides later by another post and rail up out of the dip. This was quite a big upright for a Pre-Novice and again it was sited downhill. Although it asked the same kind of question as the palisade drop, the fact that it was not filled in and that it was more upright made it a more difficult fence. You could afford to attack the palisade drop more as the take-off point was not so critical, whereas here you needed to be more accurate and balanced to get a safe jump. Heavy going and a downhill approach encourages the horse to 'prop' with his front legs, in an effort to balance himself, so he is already, in effect, backing himself off the fence and is in a good position to pull himself up completely if he wishes; the rider must organise himself into a strong riding position

at this sort of fence, and must ride with more determination than usual so as to insist that the horse keeps going forwards and tackles the fence.

'The next combination was only jumped by the Novices: a corner, followed by a stride to an upright, all made out of birch hedges. This was quite imposing for a Novice fence, but was very educational as it is exactly the sort of thing that competitors might expect to meet as they progress up through the grades. In the photo sequence the rider is obviously very determined and has risen to the challenge successfully, which in all fairness is the main priority. But, starting with the first picture, I would have liked to have seen her lower leg further forwards on the girth, so that her weight

was down in her heel. The horse looks as if he is just starting to bulge his right shoulder and is perhaps thinking about running out; if the rider's lower leg had been further forwards it would have helped her to control the horse's shoulder.

'She also needed to take up slightly more contact in the right rein, again to hold the shoulder in. If a rider tries to stop a potential run-out by pulling the opposite rein, he actually allows the shoulder to bulge out further; what he needs to do is to get the horse slightly bent towards the direction he is hanging towards. So here, with her right leg on the girth, and a little more contact in the right rein, the horse would effectively have been bent around the right leg making it almost impossible for him to escape through the right shoulder.

'As they take off, the rider has got the contact back in the right rein and they are looking straighter. But again she needs to get her weight down in the heel and her lower leg further forwards. She has adopted a good position in the air: her upper body is balanced over the horse, she has released with the arms so as not to restrict him, and both horse and rider are focussed on the next element. She does well through the rest of the combination, too, always giving the horse the freedom he needs to jump. However, all the way through she has tended to have her weight in her knee and is gripping with that, which allows the lower leg to swing back. To be even more effective, and safer, she needs to push the lower leg forwards, and to grip when necessary with her calves, not the knee. But all credit to this pair who went on to finish second.

'The Helsinki steps towards the end of the course were jumped by both the Pre–Novice and the Novice horses. At this stage I knew that my Pre-Novice horse, George, was beginning to tire in the heavy ground so as we approached I made an extra effort to make sure that his back end was really working and that he wasn't leaning on my hand. Your main aim is always to give the horse an enjoyable experience, and especially a young horse, so you should never put him in a situation where he is likely to make a mistake, but must help him to produce a good jump.

'The photo shows clearly that, having closed my lower leg and pushed George up together on the approach, he is light in front and is now focussed on the jump ahead, although as he takes off he does trail his off foreleg a little. This may have been due to the slope of the ground, or because he was tired, but it is more likely to be because I have got too far in front of him on take-off and have loaded his shoulders with my weight which, at that point, he could have well done without. On landing I have regained my position, and have closed my lower leg to help support him and pick him up. My shoulders are elevated and I am looking up and ahead, all of which helps the horse to lift himself out of the heavy ground, particularly as here George has landed quite steeply – I am in a good position to help prevent him getting bogged down in the mud and stumbling forwards.

'Both George and Cruiseway, my other ride, handled this course well; I had expected them to, because although they are green, they are both very talented horses with tremendous scope and ability. It is really just a case of introducing them to new sights and experiences. However, even a talented horse will sometimes baulk at a new question; though if you can keep him going forwards, and stay in balance with him so that when he does jump it is a pleasant experience for you both, then it is all good education for him. A good horse will respond by learning from the experience and should show improvement next time out.'

Richard Caldecott

LONGLEAT

'With our Pre-Novice course we wanted to produce an encouraging track; it shouldn't be that easy, but we make sure that the more demanding fences are not too technical, and that they have a straightforward alternative. At this level, horse and rider want to learn something from completing the course, but they also want to be encouraged.

'Our Novice course, on the other hand, is intended to be more demanding. I think some of the Novice courses these days are too easy, and would class ours as being of medium severity. I like galloping courses with plenty of room, and although the undulations here mean there is quite a pull from the water up to the top of the main hill, after that the terrain is not too demanding.

'Our course design is a result of ideas put forward by myself, as well as our technical advisers, who have included Mike Etherington-Smith, Anthony Ffooks and Jonathan Warr.

'The curved palisade is the first real question on the course because of its downhill approach and the drop on landing. For the Pre-Novices, the fence is purposely sited just back from the downhill slope so that there is barely any drop on the landing side, but for the Novices it becomes more of a "ski-jump" type fence because of the greater drop on landing.

'The post-and-rail drop in and out was Jonathan's idea. It is the first year that we have used it, and it did just sort out the less brave riders! Although both fences were numbered separately it did need to be treated like a double, and because of the drop it resembled a shallow sunken road. It was the first element that caused the trouble and it was really down to riders not being quite determined enough, or not giving their horses time to sight both elements and to work out what they were meant to be doing.

'The brush corner to the upright, along with its two other options, was my design. I wanted a feature fence for our sponsors, Manulife, and was looking for a shape that resembled an "M". You can see this fence as you come down the drive to the event, so I particularly wanted it to be an impressive complex, to set riders thinking before they even got out of their lorries! So I drew up the plan and Mike Etherington-Smith went through it with me; last year it looked more impressive because it was completely filled in with birch. As it costs about £600 to replace the birch, this year we had to make do with filling in between the jumpable parts of the fence with fir trees, which always wilt a bit – but money has to come into these things. It offers three different routes, all of which get used, which is what I had hoped for.

'We are lucky here in that we have plenty of room in which to lay out our fences, and terrain which lends itself to the flowing, galloping courses which I want to feature.'

This proved to be a good Novice course, not too demanding, but with enough there for a rider to feel he had achieved something with his horse. For George and Cruiseway it was their first Novice event, and Leslie also rode Missy (Best by Miles) there. Leslie now takes up the account:

'The first combination was a double with a one-stride distance, the fence in being an open sharks' teeth and the second element a straightforward set of rails. This was a perfectly fair fence, although with a young or green horse it was important to be aware that there was quite a lot for him to look at; he needed to be kept in balance, but also moving forwards and in front of the leg the whole time. In this sort of situation his first instinct will be to try and have a look, and so he will be tending to drop back a bit on the way to the fence – you have to be ready for this.

'I was particularly conscious of this with

Cruiseway, seen tackling this fence in the pictures; he is a very good jumper but is probably more "looky" than the average horse. However, with experience and a bit of hunting I think he will be very good because he is totally genuine. So my main aim was to keep him in front of the leg and up to the bridle, and in a positive rhythm – I wanted to maintain the same momentum and rhythm all the way to the fence. At the sharks' teeth fence I opted to jump in the middle of the V because the rails then help to keep the horse straight and also encourage him to pick up in front; it has the same effect as using schooling poles at home. Once we were in the air over the second element I took hold of Cruiseway with my left hand to start to turn him, because the course swung sharply left-handed after this fence.

'To turn a horse in the air, make sure you do this through the contact, otherwise he will resist and hollow over the fence; it is no good grabbing hold of him and pulling him one way or the other – make a turn in mid-air in the same way as you would ride a turn in the dressage arena. By teaching the horse to turn in mid-air at Novice level, he will be well prepared for when he is asked to do this over bigger obstacles when he upgrades. It is a very good way of saving both time across country, and strain on his legs; fast cross-country times are not gained by simply galloping faster between fences.

'The next fence was an upright, to a sheep feeder to an upright, again all on one-stride distances. The fences were angled in an arc shape so competitors couldn't tackle them in a straight line; thus by showing the horse how to turn in the air at the previous fence, a rider was preparing him for this fence which was slightly more complicated. The picture clearly shows this rider asking the horse to turn in the air over the second element, without it upsetting the horse's technique over the fence. A combination like this is very educational because the fences are small enough to be forgiving if horse or rider don't get it quite right, but they still teach the principle of jumping and turning. I treat fences like this as a stepping-stone towards greater things; as far as I am concerned the Novice course is not the be-all and end-all, but is a means of preparing my horses for the higher levels.

'Later on the course was an inviting double of shaped birch hedges, situated off a turn after a run down a long avenue of trees; competitors had to turn round one of the trees to get straight for the first hedge. There was very little room from the turn to the fence, and that was where the challenge of this fence lay: after the long gallop down the avenue a rider needed to balance and collect his horse in readiness to make the turn towards the fence. As you made the turn the horse needed to focus on the hedge straightaway, as it came up very quickly. Missy is shown jumping in over the first hedge, and in the second picture she looks really good – she is focussed on the fence, although I would have liked to have seen my upper body a bit further back, ready to push her forwards had it been necessary. She throws a big jump over the second hedge and I have sat back and slipped the reins so as not to restrict her. In the last picture we have landed and taken a stride, and this just shows how quickly you can pick the horse up and get it back in a rhythm and covering the ground again; and you need to if you want to achieve good times across country.

'In the next picture sequence I am jumping the Normandy bank on George. Again, the priority on the approach is to lighten the horse's front end and get him focussed on the fence. George is only five and this was his first Novice event, so I wanted to be sure that he made a good jump up onto the bank as this would then give him no choice but to bounce out over the logpile. I didn't want a tentative jump up onto the bank, which would have given him room to think about putting in a stride and either stopping, or getting very close to the logpile. So on the last few strides I have sat down into the saddle, kept myself behind the movement, and driven him forwards very positively up to the bank. We succeed in jumping well up onto the bank, and by staying behind him and closing the lower leg he knows to pick up straightaway and jump out over the logpile without hesitation. Riding the fence like this ensures there is no room for doubt in the young horse's mind about what he is expected to do. He would probably have got away with a quiet jump onto the bank and then fiddling in a short stride to the logpile, but this would have made the combination harder than it needed to be for him.

'At the end of the course was a very educational Novice fence: two angled arrowheads. The alternative was to jump the right-hand arm of the first arrowhead, and the left-hand arm of the second arrowhead. There was a big birch tree on either side of each fence which narrowed them down even more; and to add to the challenge the combination was sited on its own in the middle of a big open field. The main thing here with a novice horse is to make sure he has focussed on the fence from far enough away, so it is important to ride with a stronger and tighter contact than usual so as to hold him really straight; this also helps you to feel immediately any tendency to bulge one way or the other. However, it is equally important to keep him moving forwards, so you must not use so much hand that you prevent the back end from coming through.

'It is very easy when you come into these narrow fences to tip the upper body too far forwards; it is as though, psychologically, once you are within "range of the arrowhead target" you try to get yourself over it as quickly as possible while still on your line. In practice, of course, tipping your body forwards too soon does in fact give the horse a chance to duck out or to stop!'

Diana Pritchard Johnson

STONELEIGH

'My aim when I design a course is that the best of horse and rider should win because of their combined skill, versatility and ability, with the element of luck kept to a minimum. I also want every competitor to gain significant benefit from riding this particular course while at the same time keeping the number of eliminations to a minimum.

'To achieve this balance I need well thought out alternatives for the more demanding obstacles, using subtle angles and precise placement of fences to encourage the rider to think his way very carefully through the course at the course-walking stage. Competitors who amble round glancing at fences (sometimes from a distance) just to familiarise themselves with the route are in for a surprise when they come to ride one of my courses.

'One of the more demanding combinations here at Stoneleigh is a set of open sharks' teeth to an upright set of rails with one stride between. It is a fence which is really more of an Intermediate standard with Novice dimensions. It is situated about halfway round the course so the horses are up and running by then but, because of the size of the question being asked (a spread into an upright is certainly not simple), the alternative here costs very little extra time. I don't want an inexperienced horse tackling something he might not be ready for because the rider is afraid to loose too much time. Other fences, which require strong riding rather than technical expertise, have alternatives which waste precious seconds.

'The combination that follows the sharks' teeth is a triple with a hayrack as the central element. The hayrack attracts they eye and attention of the riders, but the real question of the obstacle is in the third element, an innocent set of rails, which is angled to invite a run-out for those not concentrating.

'There is a Normandy bank which can be ridden in about five different ways each asking a different question – as always the easiest route takes the longest time. This comes near the end of the course and the rider must assess which route to take depending upon how the horse has been performing so far. Accordingly it is wise to study all the options at the course-walking stage – some competitors only notice two out of the five alternatives and might miss an opportunity to teach their horse something new.

'The main purpose of the arrowhead at the end of the course is to slow the horses as they come to the finish. The BHS are always stressing that every effort must be made to stop horses galloping flat out through the finish into the public areas. This fence serves two purposes: it steadies the horse and makes the riders concentrate hard on the obstacle itself rather than the finishing posts only 25 yards beyond. This seems to have worked well and many a competitor has paid the price, after a good round, of being over-confident and coming at this one too fast. Again, as this is a more demanding fence than it looks, the alternative is not very time consuming – especially if you have originally decided to play safe and take that route.

'As a designer, I learn something new every time the course is ridden. There are no dress rehearsals and you cannot be sure how a fence will jump until the day of the event. For example, in 1994 I put a new set of rails at the top of the bank before the water. This asked the horses to jump into trees followed by a steep bank, with plenty of water visible from the approach. An angled alternative allowed the competitor to avoid the sight of the water and the drop. I was anxious to see how this would jump and was delighted when it worked out well, however what I had not anticipated was the determination of the riders' who took the alternative to loose as little time as possible by turning sharply upon landing to rejoin the faster track. This necessitated yanking on the horse's mouth quite considerably, which I did not enjoy watching. Similarly, the new route into the water needed a sharp left turn upon landing to line up for the log on the bank. I had envisaged horses coming gently down the bank and dropping into the water at a jog which would give them plenty of space in which to manage the turn. Although the more experienced riders achieved this perfectly, the bolder horses came onto the scene strongly and were rewarded for their courage by a sharp yank to negotiate the turn. This sort of thing can only be learned from watching horse after horse go by, then it's back to the drawing board to work out the improvements.

'I watch every fecne on the course being jumped and rely a lot on intelligenct feed-back from the fence judges. There is no room for complacency and always room for new ideas and challenges for the discerning riders.

'I would summarise by saying that I want the inexperienced to get round safely while learning a lot at the same time and to give the Open Novice competitors, and Novices ready to up grade, a challenging round with a sense of achievement for everyone at the end. Most of all I like to see intelligent course-walking and riding rewarded by a rosette.

SAVERNAKE FOREST

Savernake provides an excellent galloping course which helps to teach the Novice horse to stay in a rhythm and jump out of his stride. It is like a mini Advanced course in that it contains Novice-sized versions of everything that you will meet as you progress through the grades. It is the sort of course that will teach something to Novice horses of varying experience, and Leslie always tries to enter as many of his horses as possible here.

The first real question came at fence 6, and involved two upright logpiles set at 90° to each other. It wasn't possible to tackle them on a straight line as two angled fences because the positioning did not allow this; competitors had to jump the first one, land and then turn left-handed to the second. Leslie found plenty to observe on this, and the rest of the course:

'As you see in the photos, Matt Ryan jumps the first element right by the red flag to give himself as much room as possible to make the turn. He is in a super position, having stayed behind the movement so that he is able to assess the situation and judge the turn to the next fence. He has released with his arms so that he does not restrict the horse at all, yet has maintained contact so that in the air he has already started to take hold of the left rein, and is looking left, to indicate to the horse that he must land and turn. The horse has responded by turning smoothly and without resistance to the next element. The turn has taken two strides, and Matt has been able to ride the horse positively forwards and straight to the second element. Throughout this combination he has ridden the horse very sympathetically but also positively – this was quite a difficult fence for novice horses and riders, but Matt has made it look easy.

'Problems developed here for riders who landed and then grabbed hold of the horses' heads to pull them round the turn; the horses resisted by throwing their heads up and running away from the left rein, and were then able to run out to the right of the fence. An easier, though slower route here involved jumping the first logpile and then swinging out to the right before turning back in to jump the second element.

'The next fence was a trakehner which came after quite a long, slightly downhill gallop; the horses jumped up onto rising ground, and several had a good look at it – few seemed to get a really nice jump over it. The lip of the rising ground may have created a false groundline which would have made it harder for a horse to judge the fence.

'At this sort of fence it is important to keep the horse's head elevated a little more than usual, so that he is almost above the bit; this prevents him from peering down into the bottom of the ditch. It is also important that the *rider* doesn't look down into the bottom of the fence, but looks out and over it to where he intends going; this will encourage the horse to look up and over the fence, too, and the ditch will become a lot less noticeable.

'This sort of fence can be approached with quite a bit of pace because the ditch will hold the horse off the log, and as most horses will back themselves off this type of fence anyway, the rider needs to be sure that, once it has done this, he still has sufficient

pace to jump it. It is the sort of fence which might not give you a great feel and which might leave the horse feeling a little rattled. In this situation it is important to reassure him by giving him a pat as you gallop away, just to tell him that it wasn't his fault, he didn't do anything wrong, it was just the way that fence jumped.

'I rode Missy (Best by Miles) round the Novice course; it was the mare's third Novice, and I knew she was still a bit green at water. The water complex involved jumping over a hanging log on the bank, positioned two or three strides from the pond that you had to go into; the alternative was a log at right-angles to the direct route. When I walked the course I felt that Missy really would benefit from attempting the direct route, providing we managed it successfully. I was confident that she wouldn't actually stop, as long as I could hold her straight to the fence. So my plan of action was to come in by

the arm of the alternative so that this would help hold her into the fence – then all I had to do was concentrate on riding her forwards. I was also confident that, at worst, she would swerve off to the side, in which case she would jump the alternative.

'As we come round the corner to the log she has already started to have a look and I have got to work on her, sitting deep, driving with my arms, legs and seat. She soon gets the message that we are going, and we are off! She has started to go forwards herself, except that when she sees the water below the log, she swerves off to the right to avoid it. As I had planned, this meant she jumped the alternative, and so we didn't incur any penalties. However, as soon as she landed I had to take a very strong hold with the left rein to get back on line so that we entered the water between the red and white flags: it looks a bit ugly but we achieved our aim. Once through the complex she was happy to go forwards again, focussed on the exit.

'So on the day we got the job done, and this shows the importance of knowing your horse and considering its strengths and weaknesses when you walk the course. If Missy had taken on the direct route, that would have been fantastic, but I knew she might find it a bit much and so had plan B up our sleeves. However, she was presented with the sort of question she is going to get asked time and time again, and learnt that she must keep going and jump. Now, though, we must go home and work on teaching her to jump straight when faced with water. It isn't enough to have scraped through without penalties; next time the alternative may not be there, and she must learn to take on the question that she is faced with. But overall I felt she probably learnt more by being faced with the direct route, even though she did go off our line, than she would have done if I had opted to ride the alternative right from the start. She learnt something, but not everything and so the lesson needed to be brought home to her fully by a cross-country schooling session over a similar question.

'A little further on the course was a double of angled rails, one stride apart, the alternative to which was a big, but very fair corner; both fences were sited under some trees and at the top of a short, steep incline. When I walked the course I didn't even consider taking the alternative; the corner was wide but the top was filled in, and horses usually manage a nice big powerful jump when they have a short uphill approach to a fence –

it acts a bit like a ramp. I honestly felt the corner was a better option than the alternative, and that the risk of making a mistake at it was very low, whereas having two fences to jump can run you into more trouble than taking on a single, if more imposing-looking question.

'In the picture sequence the rider has completely lost her lower leg position coming over the first

'When riding at Pre-Novice and Novice level it is most important to use your head about what you and your horse are ready to do; though equally it is important to make sure you gain competition experience over corners, arrowheads, jumps straight into water and so on if you want to progress. Otherwise you will suddenly find yourself at Intermediate level, still not able tackle these fences, and faced with too big a question and quite possibly no alternative.

'The second to last fence was a combination consisting of two curved rails, each starting with an arrowhead-type face and then curving away so that the arm provided the alternative. The direct route meant jumping the two narrow faces which were two strides apart, and the challenge was whether or not you could hold your horse on a straight line for the approach and achieve the two strides between so as to jump out successfully. It is exactly the type of fence you would expect to meet at a higher level, element of the double; as a result she has no means of supporting or balancing herself and has virtually been jumped out of the saddle. From this precarious position she has then turned the horse to the second element, but since she is still far from secure in the saddle the horse has had no drive or support from the lower leg and has refused, almost decanting his rider completely. In fact the rider has shown grim determination in trying to carry on,

having got into such trouble at the first element, and it can only have been sheer will-power which stopped her coming off completely at the second element; but they have picked up 20 penalties. So if you learn nothing else from this book other than the importance and need for a strong lower leg position, you will already be halfway towards mastering successful cross-country riding!

only then the dimensions will be greater. So it is worth making the effort to rise to the challenge; it is infuriating if you have a glance-off and pick up 20 penalties, particularly if you were well placed after the showjumping.

▲   'In the picture sequence the horse has jumped the first element very straight, and with the rider in a good position; both have their eyes focussed on the second element. They maintain their balance, and

their line, to jump out over the second element. This is the sort of combination which requires the same balance, control and precision which you would use when jumping an in-and-out in the showjumping phase, and it was vital to have achieved this degree of control and balance on the approach to this fence – always harder to find after you have been galloping for four or five minutes. On the approach I was thinking of and feeling for: a good, strong, showjumping canter.'

Aldon provides a very good 'beginning of the season' outing for horses at all levels; the undulating countryside questions the rider's ability to balance and control his horse, but the fences themselves are not too demanding. The course features several combinations where accuracy is demanded, but as the fences are not too big a horse's confidence should be boosted because he will almost certainly be able to complete the course. There are sufficient alternatives to suit the first-timer; and even if you were unlucky and had a run-out, which would be quite easy with an inexperienced horse, you would still finish feeling you had taken a step forward rather than back.

Leslie was riding four horses round the Intermediate track: for Welton Ambassador and Envoy it was the second event of the new season, but it was a first outing for Booze Cruise and Chessman. Ambassador had been competing at Advanced level the previous year, and so it was hoped Aldon's course would serve as an easy introduction to the new season before he tackled an Advanced track a couple of weeks later. Booze Cruise and Envoy were both still at Intermediate level and would continue to compete at that level for some time. Chessman was ready to upgrade to Advanced providing he had a good trip round Aldon.

'I was pleased with all the horses' performances, but in particular with Booze Cruise. This was his first outing since his two-star three-day event last autumn; that had been his biggest challenge to date, and you can never be quite sure how a horse is going to react when you bring him out again. Some will have improved in leaps and bounds, while others may take a bit of reassuring that they can cope with what is being asked of them. At Aldon Booze felt a better horse than he was the year before, and of all of them, he was the one who felt most ready to go up a stage – it was as if he cantered round saying "Come on, this is a doddle!"'

Leslie and Booze Cruise negotiating the Sunken Road at Aldon

71

▲

The first combination on the course came after six inviting, straightforward fences so horse and rider had had time to settle into a good rhythm. As Leslie explained: 'You had to drop down two steps (on a bounce distance) and then jump an arrowhead after a distance which walked two strides; but because you had to bounce down the steps, by the time the horse landed off the second step he might have got quite steep and deep, and so wouldn't really be *going* anywhere – this made the two-stride distance to the arrowhead very long. On approaching the step the rider needed to elevate the shoulders, drop the weight down into the heel, and keep the legs closed on the girth; all in order to balance the horse, slow him down a little but *still keep him in front of your leg* so that he jumped off and down the step without hesitating. A horse will generally "back himself off" a drop-type fence, and so you need to maintain a strong lower leg to keep him going forwards.

'Once the horse has started to jump off the top of the first step you must fix your eyes on the arrowhead – it is surprising how much influence the rider's line of vision has on the horse: if *you* are looking out and ahead, it will encourage the horse to jump out and to keep his front end more upright, which in this case will make it easier for him to pick himself up as he lands at the bottom of the second step and to propel himself forwards again. By looking up and focussing on the arrowhead you are also helping your own balance – once you look down, it is easy for your body to prop forwards and your lower leg to slide back. And keeping your eye on the arrowhead is obviously going to help you keep the horse straight.

'Once you have landed off the second step you must really ride for the two strides to the arrowhead; and it is important to keep the contact as you send the horse forwards so that he stays straight and balanced, and then the rider can help him off the ground with his hand if needed.

'Ambassador has a very long stride and found the distance easy, but my other three horses all put in three strides to the arrowhead. Sometimes in a

combination with a distance like this, where you know your horse may find the two strides, for example, very long, it pays to check him a little and to hold for the three strides; however, my personal experience of this particular fence – where the horse will be very much on his forehand having come down the steps – has shown that it is best to ride for the two strides and to leave it to the horse to find room for the third stride if that is what he wants to do. The only time I have had a run-out here is when I actually held for three strides, and the horse just ducked out; so my reaction now is always to land and ride for two strides.

'If I was riding the same four horses round this course next year, I would expect them all to take on this fence in two strides. Another season's experience, as well as the benefit of some Advanced runs, would equip them with the extra confidence and scope needed to tackle the fence off two strides.

'The next "question" was a combination consisting of a bounce of upright rails, followed by a stride to another rail. It was as straightforward as this type of fence can be because it was sited on flat ground and the distances were fair. As the picture shows, the rider has balanced the horse and "set him up" with enough contained energy and impulsion to tackle the bounce fence, and this has given them a good jump in. A good leg position and steady contact has been maintained throughout. One slight complication at this particular fence is that when approaching it, you have turned back towards home, and this can encourage the horse to be a little strong coming into it. To counteract this, sit up, and close the leg and hand to push him up together which tells him to concentrate. However, this fence always seems to jump well and really it shouldn't feel any different to jumping a similar grid at home, as long as you have sufficient control and the horse's attention.

'A double of zig-zag rails one stride apart was the next question: you had to choose whether to come in at right-angles to the fence when you would have to jump the pointed part of the zig-zag; or to jump up or down through it in which case you would have to take the rails at an angle. Jumping down through it was the most direct route as far as time was concerned, but then the rails you wanted to jump had a fir tree planted halfway along them, so you had to be more accurate about the line you chose. However, this is the option I took on all my horses, and here Chessman tackles it.

'Before you got to this fence you had to come down a steep hill and then turn towards the combination, which was still on a bit of an incline. So the crucial stage when taking on this fence is the approach: in the picture it is clear that in the final stage of his approach the horse is balanced, he has elevated his front end and is focussed on the fence – before this he was still running a bit free and didn't really know where he was going next. Once you have the horse balanced and focussed, jumping the fence is easy; but if you allow him to run into this type of fence on his forehand he probably won't be able to pick his front legs up cleanly enough, and may hit the rail with one or both legs – and then you are in all kinds of trouble.

'The water complex involved a downhill approach to a log drop into the water, followed by a jump out over a log and then a long one-stride distance to a rail. Once again the priority is to balance the horse and get him off his forehand; it is vital to keep the horse in front of your leg, because although you don't want too much pace, you *do* need power and impulsion, and also to be certain that when you ask the horse to go forwards he will go.

'Having had Envoy balanced and focussed on the obstacle (see photographs), I have then allowed him to escape through the left shoulder; as a result we are not as balanced and organised as we should be, and this has given him a chance to have a bit of a look at the log drop. In my efforts to ensure that he does actually take off and jump the log, I have allowed my upper body to tip too far forwards; I should have kept my weight back and driven him forwards with my legs and seat, rather than trying to drive him on with my shoulders and arms as well. Once we are in the air I have recovered my position, but as we land in the water I have not sat back anything like far enough and have been pulled forwards over his neck, giving him the opportunity to drift left again. Now I have to work very hard to recover my balance and sense of direction to make

sure we come out of the water correctly. Envoy has fallen back into trot, so although we are now back on course we are lacking some forward momentum. Also, jumping out of the water from trot makes it a very long distance to the rail, and so Envoy has chipped in a second stride and had to make a real effort to clear the fence. This all goes to show just how important it is to keep the horse straight on the approach and throughout a combination.

'Every so often Envoy does drift left on his approach to a fence, and it is something we work on a lot at home. The approach to the water was off a right-hand bend and in this situation it is quite easy for the horse to drift out through the left shoulder. When working Envoy on the flat at home we concentrate on softening him to the left, and use grids with centring poles to encourage him to jump straight.

'The other three horses gave me a better ride through this combination as they all went in straight. Booze broke into trot in the water, however, and so he, like Envoy, had to pop in a second stride before jumping the final rail.

'Following straight on from the water was a sunken road complex: a drop down a step, and a bounce down another into the bottom of the sunken road, followed by a stride to a step up and then a bounce up the next step. In the same way as for the steps down which came earlier in the course, it is important to bring the upper body back to help balance the horse, whilst keeping the lower leg closed on the girth to keep the horse going forwards so that he can't dither at the top of the first step – you must be ready to give him a kick with your heels, or even a slap with the stick to push him off the top before he has a chance to stop. Once he tackles the first step his own momentum helps send him down the second one.

'As Booze Cruise descends the steps I have sat back, and have also slipped the reins to allow him the freedom of his head and neck; however, only

slip the reins as far as you have to – you should still maintain a contact so you can guide and balance the horse. To help him travel fluently through the combination you must encourage him to really jump *out* when he comes off the second step, as this will help him make up some of the distance in the bottom of the sunken road – I clicked to Booze and really closed the lower leg hard to tell him to jump *forwards*, rather than just dropping down off the step. Then I sat down and rode hard for the one stride to the steps up.

'We still didn't make up quite as much distance as I would have liked in the bottom of the sunken road, so Booze had to stand off the first step up,

which in turn made it a real effort to bounce up the second step. I have kept the contact as he jumps up the steps so that I can balance him and help him off the ground with my hand. It is important to keep your weight behind the horse so that you are not weighing down his front end when he tries to take off; but then you need to fold your body forwards and release with your arms to allow him to use his neck and front end fully as he goes up.

'By the time Booze cleared the final step up he had almost completely run out of impulsion and wasn't really going anywhere: and in this sort of

situation it is vital that you are there in balance with him, and have picked up the contact to help support him; you can allow him a stride or two to recover, but then it is time to say "Come on boy, let's get back in our stride and get on". By being quick to pick the horse up and to re-establish your rhythm you can save a lot of time across country without having to travel at excessive speed.

'Mark Todd riding the stallion Mayhill shows perfectly how to tackle the next combination, a right-handed corner followed by one stride to a left-hand corner. On the approach to such a fence you must balance the horse by closing the lower leg to get his hocks underneath him – you want accuracy and impulsion rather than pace. As Mark shows, it is important to elevate your shoulders, sink your weight into the heel, and keep your lower leg closed on the girth. He keeps the rein contact throughout the sequence so that he can instantly correct any thoughts the horse may have of deviating off his chosen line. On landing over the first corner Mark has dropped back into a good, secure position so that he does not get in front of the horse; by keeping your weight behind the horse you encourage and enable him to jump well as you are not hindering him by being out of balance. The whole way through this sequence Mark has his eyes fixed on the line he wants to ride: simply by looking in the right direction the rider has a great influence over where the horse goes; and by looking up and ahead a rider also corrects his own balance and position.

'On Envoy, a less experienced horse than Mark's Mayhill, I had to work harder to make the one stride between the corners. Over the first element Envoy has jumped up very high and landed quite steeply, and this has, in effect, lengthened the

distance to the next corner. As a rider it is important that you learn to feel what sort of a jump you have into a combination so that you can react immediately should the horse need help on its way out; in this particular situation I was aware we had a

lot of ground to make up so I have sat down and really driven Envoy forwards for the one stride. In my efforts to pick him off the floor at the point of take-off, to make sure that he doesn't try to chip in a second stride, I have got my weight too far forwards – but we have achieved our purpose! The other horses, including the less experienced Booze Cruise, all found the distance easy, but they tend to have a looser jump than Envoy and would have made up more distance in the air over the fence.'

The Batten Family

ALDON

Mary Thomson and King William tackle the water complex

Aldon Horse Trials started in 1980 as just a Novice track; since then an Intermediate and Pre-Novice course has been added. The event is hosted, organised, and the course designed and built by the Batten family. 'Our daughter Bridget was a keen competitor and we were aware of the need for more events in the spring. As our Aldon estate is sited on Yeovil sand we knew that we would be able to offer good going whatever the weather; a mid-March date suited out family commitments and has also meant that we attract Badminton-bound horses who are able to run in the Open Intermediate section,' explains Mr Batten.

'Various members of our family and friends provide ideas for new fences; it's then down to my son David and I to sort out which might turn into a practical obstacle. Since we started the event there has been a tremendous improvement in the standard of horses, and the skill of the riders. The rule book sets out the acceptable fence dimensions and it is fair to say that, in the absence of any awkward topographical features, the measurements are such that, in the case of straightforward single fences, the horse can jump them without any great difficulty.

'Within the family we each seem to have adopted our own particular role: David tries hard to produce new, interesting and horse-testing combinations; his mother concentrates on calming him down; while I have to decide how the obstacle can be built so as to cope with several hundred horses jumping it on the day.

'We are one of the first events of the season and this fact colours our thinking on course design. A course consists of a maximum/minimum permitted number of "efforts"; we feel the first three or four fences should be straightforward, and the remainder should be an even mixture of single fences and combinations; you should aim to have one, or possibly two, straightforward fences after a testing combination.

'We feel very strongly that the line the course takes is of utmost importance; the course should flow like a stream of water, with no awkward corners or twists. Fences should be angled so that, on landing, horse and rider are well positioned for the next obstacle. We do not plan to make the course harder each year, but we like to incorporate a few new fences each time. It is very difficult to think of original ideas for fences – the much admired bank complex introduced in 1994 was the result of an awful lot of thinking over the last two years.

'We like to design the course to test for accurate riding and the nerve of the jockey. By staying within permitted dimensions, all horses should be able to jump a clear round, so we try to include a fence which is a "jockey scarer" or which requires the rider to have the horse under sufficient control so as not to have a run-out. We don't want to see too many eliminations so we try to set the standard to match the average ability of the horses/riders who will be taking part – both should enjoy the ride. Horses do not like going downhill to a fence, nor do they appreciate landing into rising ground (such as the old Becher's Brook in the Grand National). Occasionally you get a fence which is unexpectedly *unsuccessful* and which causes a lot of problems; this is almost always due to a quirk of the terrain. When designing a course you have to remember this; if the terrain is unfriendly simply lowering the height of the fence will not actually make the fence easier.

'We run Aldon in aid of the RNLI and other charities, and a good financial surplus is important to us. For this reason you do not see fences here which are particularly "fancy" or which have incurred much expense on peripheral "tarting-up" and scenery; but the fences are substantial and well built, which is usually what horse and rider appreciate most.

'Things do not always work exactly as you had planned; sometimes riders see how a fence can be jumped in a way which we had not envisaged, as shown by the following examples.'

EXAMPLE 1   1993

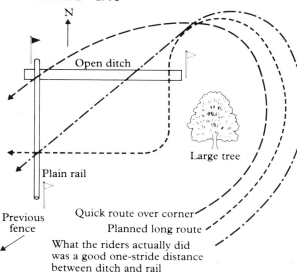

Previous fence

Quick route over corner

Planned long route

What the riders actually did was a good one-stride distance between ditch and rail

EXAMPLE 2 The Fish Hook 1993

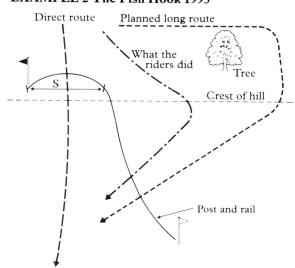

1994

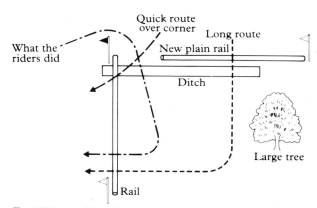

For 1995 we will probably site an extra fence to the NE so that the competitors have to skirt round the tree

The Fish Hook 1994

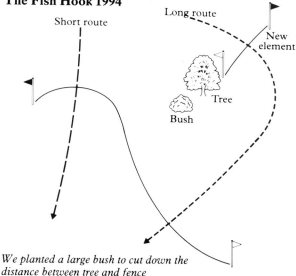

We planted a large bush to cut down the distance between tree and fence

Poplar Park is another popular, early season event, with inviting courses and good, sandy going. It was a first outing of the season for Haig, Leslie's Badminton-bound ride, and he was also riding Ambassador and Envoy; they were all to tackle the Intermediate track. The first problem on the course was the arrowhead fence positioned a good three strides from the step up out of the first water. Leslie takes up the explanation:

'In the first picture sequence the horse is ridden by Blyth Tait: as it comes out of the water, Blyth has immediately organised himself into a good balanced position, and has the horse off its forehand and with its attention on the fence ahead. He has kept it balanced on the approach and meets the fence on a good stride. After a horse has jumped out of water it sometimes takes it a stride or two to regain its balance; should this happen, by the time it actually sees the next fence it may have drifted right or left – as happens to the horse pictured in the next sequence.

'The second picture sequence shows that even as this horse comes out of the water, it is obvious that it has not got the balance and the focus that the other horse had: it is looking to the left, and by the second picture the rider is trying to correct this by pulling it back over to the right. It over-reacts, and now the rider has to pull it over to the left and keep it on line for the arrowhead.

The rider has done well in that she has managed to get the horse through the combination at all, since a runout looked almost certain. Because she has had to work so hard to keep the horse straight, she has lost her lower leg position and has therefore rather slipped up the horse's neck once he does take off. But she had a difficult job from the start, and it was easy to see where it all went wrong: instead of preparing the horse in the water so that it was focussed and listening to her as it jumped out, she didn't appear to think about the arrowhead at all until they were out of the water, by which time it was almost too late, as the horse obviously has its mind elsewhere.

'Basically, it all comes back to being able to keep the horse between hand and leg: Blyth has prepared his horse in the water; he has picked him up and balanced him and kept him going forwards, in front of his leg, both through the water and on the approach to the arrowhead.

'A new fence to the course was an 'elephant trap', a decent-sized set of rails over a big ditch, but which wouldn't normally be expected to cause a problem at this level; however, even the so-called let-up fences have to be treated with respect. In the first picture the horse jumps the fence with great confidence. It is important to keep the horse in front of the leg: with a wide fence like this you must be able to ride him right up to the base of it, so it is equally vital that when you go to press the horse up to it, that he will respond. You would probably want to keep his head a little higher than usual to prevent him looking down into the ditch, though once he takes off you follow the contact through as normal. This sort of fence used to be built as a rider-frightener, but most riders nowadays would tackle it quite confidently so it has become more of a let-up fence.

'If a horse is given the chance to look down into the ditch it may very well slam the brakes on. The

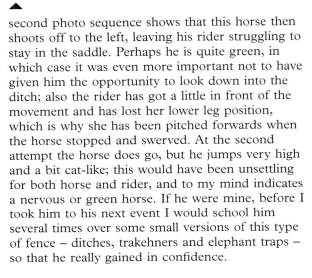

second photo sequence shows that this horse then shoots off to the left, leaving his rider struggling to stay in the saddle. Perhaps he is quite green, in which case it was even more important not to have given him the opportunity to look down into the ditch; also the rider has got a little in front of the movement and has lost her lower leg position, which is why she has been pitched forwards when the horse stopped and swerved. At the second attempt the horse does go, but he jumps very high and a bit cat-like; this would have been unsettling for both horse and rider, and to my mind indicates a nervous or green horse. If he were mine, before I took him to his next event I would school him several times over some small versions of this type of fence – ditches, trakehners and elephant traps – so that he really gained in confidence.

'The second water complex involved turning off a track to jump a log drop into water. In the first picture sequence the horse has come in very balanced, and although the rider has slipped the

reins and sat back, he has still managed to maintain the contact. On landing he has sat nice and deep, and has helped balance the horse to ride the one stride to the rails in the water; remember that a stride does not ride as easily in water as it does on dry ground, so more effort is required from horse and rider. Here, the rider has opened the left rein to keep the horse straight, which is the correct reaction should it drift off line. They get a good jump over the rails, and the rider has maintained the contact to help support and balance the horse for the step out – this was quite small, and there is a lot of spray thrown up which means it is easy for the horse not to notice it properly. This is why it is very important to keep the leg on and maintain the contact so as to encourage the horse to come up out of the water.

'Another testing question was a double of corners which walked 10 to 11 yards, or two short strides – certainly a short distance for a cross-country combination. It meant that the horse had to be

▼

brought right back, with his hocks well under him, so that he approached the first element as if he were going into a showjumping combination. For this sort of problem, whilst you want the horse to be light on his forehand, you would hold him with a stronger contact than if you were showjumping in order to keep him on your line over the corners and to support his front end, particularly if he does get close to the second element.

'In the sequence of pictures, horse and rider look very much in unison and balanced as they take off over the first corner; they are both focussed on the second element, and in the third picture the rider has sat up and held and supported the horse to back him off the second element, so they fit the two strides in comfortably. The horse looks a little bit unbalanced with his front legs, but this is probably because he found the distance a bit tight, and has tried to twist them out of the way. However, the rider helped the horse out by sitting deep and giving him a little check to keep him on his line and also to fit in two strides.

'On Envoy and Ambassador this is exactly how I rode it, but on Haig, who is a much bigger horse than the other two, things went wrong. I had a lovely jump in over the first corner, but it was perhaps a bit too big and bold; I sat and held for two strides but Haig started to pick up off one stride – he then seemed to realise I was trying to hold him back and put his front legs down again to take the second stride; but this put us right in the base of the second corner. He tried to jump it, but being so close he breasted it and fell. In hindsight, having had such a good jump in I should have taken a definite pull and then given the rein, then checked again for the second stride before releasing him to jump.

'Having checked that he was all right I took the decision to continue round the course; there were only about six jumps left, all mainly straightforward galloping ones, and I felt we both needed our confidence restoring quickly. Also, there was another straightforward corner four fences on and I was keen to give him a good jump over this, to reassure him that he could still tackle this type of fence.

'This next corner fence was big but fair, its only other possible problem being that it was in the middle of a field, so it was very open with nothing to help keep you on your line. On walking the course this had been my only concern here, and I knew that I would have to prepare the horse well in advance so that he would be focussed and concentrating on what I wanted him to jump. The first picture shows Envoy: I have got him balanced and attentive, and he is extremely aware of where we are going; he has stayed straight, and meets the fence well. There is, however, more daylight than I would like to see between me and the saddle; I should have folded up more and stayed close to the saddle. Envoy has taken off with his near fore folded up tighter than his off fore, which could be because of my position – I would be weighing his front end down.

'I had a good jump here with Haig, which pleased me; I kept a stronger leg and hand contact to provide him with some trust and confidence, trying to transmit strength and trust through me to him. I didn't push him faster, just used a stronger hand, leg and seat to hold everything together. He was very honest and tackled it confidently.'

Michael Lloyds

POPLAR PARK

'Poplar Park first ran a BHS horse trials in 1984: I had been on the committee involved in organising competitions there previously, and when the BHS approached us about running an affiliated horse trial, I was put forward as organiser. After the first year our course designer and builder left to work in the Middle East and I just took over where he left off. The staff on the farm do the actual building and, for me, the course designing can only be a hobby – much as I enjoy it I have to earn my living as well! The late Bill Thomson was our technical adviser and he taught me a great deal. He only missed one year at Poplar Park, in 1985, and Philip Herbert took his place, and Philip is our present adviser.

'The terrain here at Poplar Park means that we can't build a real galloping course. It is a mixture of grassland and semi-heath and although it is sandy, well draining soil, it is quite a dead surface for horses to have to run on. All this is borne in mind when we are designing the courses. We also have to remember that we are very early in the horse trials calendar and so the course also has to suit the fact that horses and riders will only just be getting into the swing of things.

'The first water complex is the one we started with originally, at the very first event. It has been lengthened since then and although it is not particularly difficult, it does involve jumping into darkness, which is quite daunting for a horse; and it is also running water which does bother some horses. Also the ground in that particular area of the course is not very stable, and as they jump in and out of the water the ground actually shakes, and they obviously feel this. So because of these few complications the entry and exit from the water itself is intentionally straightforward. The arrowhead was added three strides from the step out, to make the fence a little more challenging. Horses tend to jump into this particular water quite big and fast, and the rider has very little time to get himself organised once he has entered it; so those who have a controlled jump in and can keep their horse balanced have no problem riding the arrowhead, whilst those that stumble or rush tend to come out in an unbalanced and disorganised way, and it is easy to incur a runout. The arrowhead was introduced for the first time in 1993 when the rail

to be jumped was about six feet wide. This year we narrowed it down a bit to increase the degree of control and accuracy that the rider must produce.

'We built the second water complex about six years ago, with Bill Thomson advising us. He suggested we made it a good stretch of water so that we would have some flexibility should we want to add to it at a later date; originally it did not have any rails actually in the water. The log pile competitors have to jump over to get into the water is not particularly big, but it is sufficient to test the horses that are willing to take off over a fence into water, and those which have only ever been pushed off a step into water. Also the horse does not actually see the water on approach, only once he is about to jump. The rails in the water again are not particularly big, but water does hold the horse down and shorten his stride, and at this stage in the course – two-thirds of the way round – he will be starting to feel a little weary. Once he is in the water there is not much room to get gathered up and organised in order to jump the rails. So in this situation they are plenty big enough.

'The double of corners was built last year. We knew instinctively once we had completed it that the distance between the two was not quite what we had wanted, so we did put in an alternative here. The problem with cross-country fences is that they are not that easy to adjust once they have been built, but after taking advice from Philip Herbert we did leave them in as he felt they still asked a fair question. This year we moved the arms of the corners but did not move the point of them: this gave a wider 'target area' but still left us with an unusual distance. We had really intended it to be jumped on one long stride, and some tackled it that way, but the majority came in quietly and took it on two strides.' [It was at this fence that Haig fell with Leslie: having jumped in big, he tried to take off on one stride but then put down again for a second stride and breasted the corner.]

'We did put in another alternative at this fence, but still 16 per cent of the entries incurred penalties here. What did surprise us were the eliminations where riders, having had a problem riding the direct route, then did not ride the correct alternative route. I think some riders have it fixed in their minds that they are going to ride a direct route, and are not really prepared for when something goes wrong. It is important always to walk the alternative routes even if it is not your first intention to jump them. The effect this fence had on riders did surprise us, as the corners were not big even though the striding was unusual. However, it was never our intention to make the striding difficult and the fence may well be altered again for next year.

'The elephant trap was new this year and did look quite spectacular; building a fence like that over a gaping hole with no upright supports does make it look enormous, but it was actually no bigger than anything else on the course and was really just a rider frightener. The approach to it, and exit were good and it came at a point in the course where the terrain did allow us to include a big, bold galloping fence.

'As a course builder I like to include a good mix of fences; I am not a great believer in going for endless arrowheads and fences which are a test of pin-point accuracy, because I think both riders and horses get fed up with that after a while – so I try not to go too much one way or the other. Everyone can make a mistake and we do sometimes get something wrong; we don't have the opportunity here, as some courses do, of putting a few horses over the course before the event to judge how it rides, which is always useful. One year we found that several horses fell during the same afternoon at the same fence, where it had been jumped without incident in the morning. We could only guess that the horses' judgement was affected by jumping into the sun and so since then we have faced those fences in a different direction. After the problems the sport experienced in 1993, with several tragic accidents, everyone has become pretty paranoid about safety and now it is very much a case of "if in doubt, take it out".'

Jonathan Warr

STOWE

Jonathan Warr is the course designer at Stowe Horse Trials, and is responsible for the Intermediate course there. Here he describes the problems and responsibilities faced by the course designer, and what in particular he set out to achieve at Stowe:

'There are always certain things which a course designer has to consider when planning a cross-country course: first, landscape and budget; then the date of the competition, and what the organiser is hoping to achieve; and finally, liaison with other individuals involved – the organiser, the BHS technical steward and so on.

'During times of recession, organisers are generally most concerned about ensuring that they can attract maximum entries to help finance the event, and so they may prefer their designer not to be too adventurous – they just want everyone to have a good cross-country round and to have enjoyed themselves so that they will come back again the following year. So whilst the landscape, for example, may lend itself to a more technical or demanding course, you are not always given a free rein to use the terrain to its full potential in that respect.

'When I first started designing courses, the majority of riders at Intermediate and Advanced levels were more tightly grouped in terms of skill and experience. Now there is a very great span of ability, particularly at Intermediate level, and so you have to work out exactly what standard you are aiming for.

'The first question I asked was at fence 5, the double of palisades. Up until then everything had been simple and straightforward, and I felt it was soon enough in the course to put something in the riders'

way. By siting a relatively narrow fence at the bottom of a bank I am asking the rider to keep a measure of control and to be able to present his horse accurately at the obstacle. He then has to be able to achieve a relative distance to the second element. Riders often complain about arrowhead-type fences, and whilst I am not as great an advocate of them as some other designers, they do achieve a result: they make people learn to ride better and to school their horses to a higher degree of obedience. We are not allowed to make the dimensions any greater, and so we have to provide a challenge in some other way, and this is just one of the tools available to us.

'To reach the first water complex the riders had to come through a gateway and make a sharp right-hand turn; as this doesn't provide much of an approach I was reluctant to put anything too complicated in the horses' way. But at the second water I could ask a bit more; the bounce in demanded a controlled but determined approach, followed by a step out of the water with a stride to a narrow chair fence. I was pleased with how well this rode. The distance was only meant to be one stride but a few fiddled in two and the nature of the fence allowed this to work both ways.

'The bounce at the end of the course was put there to make the riders keep thinking right the way through. Had it been a straightforward fence they would have just batted on round the last section of the course without having to do too much. I think it is important for riders to have to pay as much attention to the challenges near the end of the course as at the start.'

The Intermediate course at Stowe is very well built. It is suitable for recently upgraded horses as well as the more experienced – it asks some good questions by making use of the undulating countryside, but is not too big so, given a fair ride, the horse should be gaining confidence as he makes his way round. Leslie's rides were Welton Envoy, Sidney's King, Booze Cruise and Lowenac. The younger horses, Envoy, Booze and Sid, did not have that much experience at Intermediate level; however, it was hoped that here they would acquire one of the three clear rounds that were needed to qualify for a two-star three-day event at the end of the autumn. Lowenac, on the other hand, had already completed a two-star event, Windsor, in the spring and having had a short break, was now being prepared for the Intermediate Championships at Gatcombe and a second three-day event.

The going was very good, but things did not get off to a very good start when Booze Cruise fell at the practice fence. It seems he was so neat with his front legs that he somehow got hooked up in his breastplate and couldn't get his leg free in time to land. Amazingly it did not knock his confidence at all, and he went on to jump clear. Envoy, who at that moment probably needed the most riding of the three youngsters, had a runout which Leslie felt he could have avoided: 'There was a right–hand corner fence about halfway round the course with rails off either side of the corner to form the alternative route,' he explains. 'I didn't really allow for the fact that the horse might shy away from the left-hand rails, which is what Envoy did; I should have got him in tighter to the left-hand side of the corner to allow for this happening. Apart from that he coped with the course well. Sidney's King, who is a very bold horse, took everything in his stride – yet Luke, who is the most experienced, gave me the hairiest ride, as you will see in a minute!'

Leslie's first ride was Sidney's King: 'Sid is a fairly onward-bound horse, and as many of the early fences were sited downhill I knew I was going to have to work to keep him balanced and off his forehand so that he didn't just bowl headlong into his fences. The first real test came at fence 5, a double of palisades on a one-stride distance. The fences were quite narrow and sited in the bottom of a deep hollow, so the approach involved quite a steep descent. At the top of the bank I brought Sid back to a trot. At this stage the horse is paying

more attention to the downward transition I have asked for than to what's coming next, so I make sure that I keep my eyes focussed on the fence to come. I keep my leg on and my head and shoulders up to help balance the horse; in the next photo Sid is now fully concentrating on where we are going. He has lifted his head and neck and is focussed on the fence, and this is the cue for me to start to drive him more positively forwards now that we have the necessary balance and concentration. Sid produces

a good jump over the first element and then concentrates on the second element.

'The horse had made the fence easy for me in this case; he came back when asked, and then focussed on the task ahead. The fence rode as well as I had hoped it would when walking the course. The key to riding this sort of fence well is simply to keep the horse balanced and straight on a downhill approach; a rider must keep his shoulders up so that his weight does not get in front of the horse; the weight should be down in the lower leg and heel. Aim to keep the horse's poll as the highest point – this is where flatwork training will help.

The next sequence shows another rider tackling the same complex: at the top of the bank everything looks to be in order, although the horse has just started to bulge his left shoulder, and the rider is trying to straighten this out with his right rein. As he goes on through, the rider is having to work hard to keep the horse straight, and he has opened the right rein to prevent the horse veering further to the left. The horse looks a little surprised at what is in front of him, and has been slow to pick up his front legs. The rider is taking no chances and still has a slightly open right rein, and has succeeded in straightening the horse up. The result is a much better jump over the second element; the rider was able to soften his hand to the horse on the approach which has allowed the horse to use himself properly. A good example of efficient 'corrective' riding.

Leslie continues with his own experience of the course: 'About halfway round the course came the second water complex; it was very much a "light into dark" situation, as the water was surrounded by trees. You had to jump over a rail followed by a bounce over a drop into water. There was very little room to land before the drop so you had to get the horse back into a collected canter. It was one of those situations calling for the delicate balance between the horse being controlled and collected enough to prevent him jumping in too big over the rails, and keeping the hind end engaged sufficiently so that the horse would not consider stopping. You needed to keep your weight back, ensure that the horse stayed in front of your leg, and then allow him enough length of rein so as not to restrict him over the drop. Coming out you had to tackle a decent-sized step up, followed by a long one-stride distance to an arrowhead-type chair fence. With Booze Cruise, who is a very onward-bound horse, I rode for the one stride but he really had to reach to clear the spread of the chair; on Luke and Envoy I therefore decided to settle for two strides, which seemed to give them a more comfortable jump over the chair. Asking the horse to trot, rather than canter, through the water, gave them a little bit more room to fit in the two strides.'

In the picture sequence, this horse and rider come up over the step and look to be on a good attacking stride to the chair. However, instead of picking up off one stride as the rider expected, the horse has chipped in a second, very short stride and has had to 'cat-leap' the fence. The rider has been slightly jumped out of the saddle on take-off, but has managed to get his weight back quickly, although it has meant he is restricting the horse with the reins. The horse lands very steeply over the fence, but again, the rider has been able to keep his weight back behind the horse.

Greg Watson on the other hand gets a big jump out of the water which makes it easier for the horse to go for one stride before taking off – it picks up off one stride and takes the fence on. Greg has got a little in front of the horse on take-off (and at this point a lesser horse could easily have put his front feet back down again) but the photo shows that he has regained his position and given the horse sufficient freedom of the head and neck so as not to restrict him over the spread.

Two fences later came a jump up onto a Normandy bank with a decent ditch in front of it, followed by a bounce off over some rails, making it a big drop off the other side. Here, Leslie's ride Luke shows how *not* to do it! 'Coming into the bank you needed to set the horse up as it was quite

a short distance on the top; you wanted a positive, but not too big, jump. So having got Luke back into a more collected canter, I kept my leg on for the last four or five strides, and slightly increased the pace into the fence. Once on the bank it was important to elevate the shoulders to help keep the weight back, and to help the horse off the ground with the hand to ensure he knew to bounce rather than put in a stride. Luke looks hollow on the top of the bank and then leaves a front leg behind an uncomfortable moment for both of us!'

Leslie gives an excellent demonstration in these pictures of how his position and style give his horse the maximum chance of recovery. His weight is well down into his heel and his lower leg is firm and slightly forwards, and he is allowing the horse complete freedom to stretch the head and neck, which it needs to do to counterbalance leaving a front leg behind. Throughout he maintains a light contact in case the horse needs support from the rein on landing.

'The picture of Matt Ryan shows his horse taking a bold jump off the bank; Matt has let go of the reins with one hand to give his horse the freedom he requires. He has kept his weight further back than I have, which shows how we all develop our own style.'

The second-to-last fence was a very upright bounce which followed a steady pull uphill. By this stage, over a hilly course, the horse is inevitably a bit tired and his stride has probably got long and flat. It is important to remember this when setting the horse up for such a combination as he will probably respond quite quickly to you checking him, but may not be so quick to move away from the leg again or to keep the hindquarters engaged; so when you take hold of the horse to balance him in front of the jump, you must make sure you also keep the engine running!

In the next picture sequence the rider has got in front of the horse on take-off; it has not made a very clean jump, and this could have left the rider in a vulnerable position. The rider has regained an acceptable and safe position on landing over the first element, but has again got in front of the horse on take-off, and is looking down and to the right. Getting in front of the horse on take-off can lead to

two problems: it gives the horse the chance to put his front feet back down and stop, and it is easier for the rider to be unseated if he hits the fence. This time the rider has not regained such a good position; her weight is still too far forward and her lower leg has slipped back further.

Over the same fence, Lucinda Murray's horse makes a very good shape with his front legs snapped up tightly; Lucinda stays in balance, although even she has allowed her lower leg to creep back! She lands in an ideal position, with her lower leg on the girth; she is sitting securely in the saddle and has kept a contact with the horse's mouth. She closes her legs on the girth, is very soft with her hands, and the horse responds with an excellent jump out. At this point she is not in the most secure position should anything go wrong, but you can't blame her for trusting a horse which is as neat in front as this one!

Less than a week before this event Leslie had had the splint taken off his previously broken ankle and had successfully competed an Intermediate horse at Tidworth during that week. He had intended only doing the dressage and showjumping, but having found himself well in the lead, and eager to see what his ankle could cope with, he also did the cross-country – and won! At Savernake a few days later his ankle was going to have to hold out for one Novice horse on the Saturday, and three Advanced horses on the Sunday!

On the Advanced course, the first combination was a double of curved hedges, set on two strides, with a wide ditch in front of each hedge. It asked a similar question to the double of curved rails on the Novice course, in that the direct route meant holding your line to the narrower face on each hedge. As Leslie explains: 'It walked a long two strides, which would have been fine on good ground but the rain had made the going very holding and it actually rode more like two-and-a-half strides, which is why this fence proved so influential on the day.

'To jump it successfully, it was necessary to be accelerating on the approach, which is difficult to do when you also need to establish an accurate line and distance to the first element. In the first picture sequence, horse and rider have come in very strong and have had a really good jump over the first element. However, the horse has then run slightly right-handed, which has further increased the distance to the second element; but the rider has been really strong and has kept the horse going forwards, and has made him pick up off the second stride. The horse has had to stretch himself, but because he had such a good jump over the first element he had the confidence to take the second hedge on.

'In the second picture sequence the horse is straightaway lacking acceleration going into the combination, starting to back off some way away which you really couldn't afford to do here. He has taken a look at the ditch and has then stood right off the fence and "cat-leaped" it, and because he has jumped high rather than forwards over the fence, he has only just cleared the spread. The rider knows that she has got a lot of ground to make up and has really gone for it, but they don't make up the distance – they are still too far off the second hedge and the horse has stopped. If he had had a nice jump in over the first element he may have had the confidence to stand off at the second, but he didn't and so wasn't prepared to risk it again. It may have paid the rider to have held and collected the horse to try and fit in an extra stride.

'A few fences further on came the trakehner, a very big tree trunk over a ditch; it is a very impressive-looking fence, but shouldn't cause a problem to any horse at Advanced level. It also has a slightly downhill approach, but again, as long as the horse was balanced within his gallop, he should be able to just keep running to it.

'Two fences later came the bunker fence, a big hanging tree trunk at the top of the bunker, then down into the bottom of the hollow, a turn, and out by jumping over some upright rails. The rider pictured has come in very positively and had a good jump over the tree trunk. She could have had her lower leg forwards a bit more and on the girth, especially as this is basically a drop fence. Her upper body and arm release is good, but as a result of her lower leg slipping back, her upper body has been jerked forwards a bit as the horse lands and runs down the slope. In the bottom of the bunker she has got reorganised and has managed the turn to the exit rails; she had her eyes fixed on the exit fence and has ridden positively up to it.

'I had already decided to take the longer option here, which meant jumping the tree trunk, pulling out to the left and then turning back in to tackle the rails. I was thinking a little cautiously because of my ankle injury and had decided to have a "play safe" day! On Haig I started to take hold of him with my left hand whilst still in the air over the log. We then circled round the top of the bunker so that we approached the exit rails on the flat – all I needed to do was judge my turn and keep riding him forwards to the fence. I still didn't really feel "match fit"; I wasn't sure how much strength I had in my lower leg to land over a drop fence like that and then to push the horse round the turn and up to the rails – personally, I do find security of mind in knowing that I have security in my lower leg, and I couldn't be sure I had it that day!

'The water complex looked very impressive, but for an experienced Advanced horse it wasn't too demanding: you had to jump a replica of Savernake House, followed by a forward five strides to an ascending log drop into the water. The way out was a bounce up two steps to an arrowhead, set on a forward three strides. The horse shown in the first set of pictures is being ridden positively towards the water jump; the rider's position is good, being slightly behind the movement. The horse jumps well into the water, and is particularly good with his front legs, and the rider has slipped the reins, giving him the freedom to cope with the drop. She is quick to pick up the reins and to gather the horse up for the steps – but here the horse jumps too big and bold up the first step and so lands right in front of the face of the second step. The rider has relied on

her hands to snatch him off the floor to prevent him breasting it.

'By now they have strayed off their line, and this makes the distance to the arrowhead very long. The horse stands right off this and takes his rider a little by surprise; she has tried very hard to stay with him and succeeds with her legs and upper body, but she is just off balance enough to have to hold on with her hands, and this has caused the horse to invert and jump very high. In fairness, she has done very well to get this horse through the combination; things went wrong when he jumped too exuberantly up the steps and drifted off his line. If this particular horse has a tendency to rush out of water in this way, another time it might be as well for the rider to consider bringing him back to trot in the water; had she been able to contain his jump out, she would have had far more control throughout the exit fences.

'This fence proved even more dramatic for myself and Chessman, who was tackling his first Advanced track. As the photo sequence shows, we came over the Savernake House well enough, but then I didn't ride him strongly enough towards the water. It was a forward five strides but I had decided to ride for six which, in hindsight, was wrong: it meant I landed over the house and then made a point of sitting there to hold for six strides, and this didn't take into account how much of a look the horse might take at the big fence into the water. When he suddenly started to back off, it was panic and out with the elbows and the stick! One minute I was riding on a collected stride and the next I was summoning everything I had to push the horse forwards to the fence!

'Chessman took off quite well, but I have folded up too much for this type of fence; we landed fairly steeply with the result that I was tipped too far forwards and in front of the saddle, and when Chessman just caught the top of the fence with his hind legs it was enough to tip me off altogether. I did manage to get back on, but being extremely wet I opted for the long route out, jumping up one side of the steps and then turning back to jump the arm of the arrowhead. There was a second water fence later on and I was keen both for my sake, and the horse's, that we continue and jump it if we could. I felt all right, and as Chessman hadn't fallen himself it seemed sensible to continue.

'Chessman did tackle the second complex successfully, although he was still a little slow going in, but it was good for both of us to do it. I still had two Advanced horses to ride so it was helpful to have a complete run round the course and to extract some good from what went wrong. If my leg had been at full strength I would like to think I would have stayed in the plate; luckily I managed to on the other rides!'

Mike Etherington-Smith

SAVERNAKE FOREST & BLENHEIM

Savernake: 'This course reflects how I like to try and bring all the elements I spoke about earlier into play, at Novice and Advanced level. At Savernake Novice, for example, the two palisades set around a corner were designed to test the rider's ability to make the turn and to ride the related distance between the fences. They were also slightly downhill, and involved jumping and turning left so it was easy for the rider to find himself starting to turn left too soon and giving himself a harder task. Thus the first element needed to be jumped well over on the right-hand side to get a smooth turn and approach to the second fence. The fence was harder than it looked and that is the sort of test I love, because it tests whether the rider has stopped to consider what the course designer is trying to test. There were several questions at this simple combination that needed a response: for example, can the rider hold his line; at which exact point of the fence is he aiming to jump; and can he ride accurately the related distance for the line he has chosen.

'The filled-in corner with the option of the angled rails was easier than perhaps it looked. If a fence has an alternative riders often assume that the jump that appears to be the direct route is the most difficult. In fact there wasn't a great deal of time to be saved by jumping the corner, and so the choice was really simply down to what each rider preferred to try. At Novice level it is quite unusual to have a corner sited at the top of a hill, but it wasn't a big fence, and horses always seem to jump uphill well.

'Similarly the double of curved rails was easier than it looked, but because the arms of the curve offered an option a lot of riders thought to play safe and took a longer route. In fact it was simply a double of rails on a related distance which any horse and rider should be capable of jumping safely; had I simply made it two straight post-and-rail fences in exactly the same position, no rider would have thought twice about tackling it, but introducing the option puts a measure of doubt in some riders' minds.

'At any level I am a great believer in using ditches in front of fences as this really gets horses in the air and jumping; a rider can "miss" badly at a fence like this and the ditch will still hold the horse off the fence so that he can jump safely. From a course designer's point of view ditches have another useful purpose: few horses stay straight when they jump a ditch or a big oxer, and will nearly always drift off one way or the other; so introducing ditches and oxers into combinations will test how well the rider knows his horse – which way will his horse drift, how greatly will it affect the line he wants to ride and therefore the distance to the next fence? A thinking rider will make an adjustment to his approach, or he will be ready to keep hold of the opposite rein in mid-air, or he will use an open hand, to help keep the horse on his chosen line.

'In the Advanced course at Savernake the double of curved hedges and ditches incorporated all these elements. The distance between them was a forward two, or a short three strides, but this would be altered further if a horse drifted off his line, which he would be quite likely to do when jumping over the big spread of the ditch and hedge.

'The park at Savernake is fairly featureless and so I wanted to make use of the natural bunker in it. The hanging log going in meant that the horse had to jump without knowing where he would land; though at Advanced level you would not expect this to be too much of a problem, particularly with a fence as straightforward as this. The real test was whether the rider could maintain rein contact having come in over the drop, in order to steer the horse out over the exit rails. The curve of the rails meant that if the rider wasn't organised and in control the horse would just run along the rail and miss the fence, rather than being punished by trying to jump and perhaps tipping up over it.

'The new water jump looked impressive, although at this level the jump in wasn't big; even so, there were one or two stops here. In fact it is the relationship between the jump in and then successfully coming out up the steps which is the more influential, rather than the jump itself. The majority of horses should jump in successfully, but again, the test was of the rider's ability to pick the horse up and get reorganised in the water so as to then come out over the steps well. The course budget didn't allow it this time, but next year I hope to add something to the exit combination to make it even more important that the rider is in full control coming out.

Blenheim: 'At this level a designer needs to be thinking about testing the horse and rider as well as about educating them both. I like to vary the questions a little from year to year so that it isn't too boring for regular competitors and spectators, although in 1994, because we hosted the European Young Rider Championships, I did not want to make too many changes; we would be catering for a large number of riders who had never been to Blenheim before.

'I rarely start out thinking I must change this or that unless I felt it was a bad fence – and then I hope I would have had the confidence to remove it, or change it before the actual competition. When a designer updates or modifies a course he must be aware of the relationship between fences, and how a simple change at one fence may affect several other fences on the course. For example the TNT flyer, an impressive-looking gaping ditch in front of a big brush fence, is now more of a rider-frightener than anything else; although I still make sure that somewhere before this fence is a smaller ditch, just to help prepare horse and rider. And if I decided to do away with the ditch at the earlier fence it might affect how well the TNT flyer jumped.

'If the same fence has been in use for several years then I like to change it so that it doesn't look dated – unless it is a "let-up" fence, in which case there is no point taking it out just to replace it with another straightforward fence.

'After any event where I am designing the course, when I revisit the site I try to go without any preconceived ideas – I want to be able to look at the course with a fresh pair of eyes. I often look for another route, although this is not always possible or practical. At Blenheim for example, I had thought of reversing the direction of the track as they do at Badminton, but it just doesn't feel right when you walk it the other way, and as yet I haven't found the space to produce another route that has the same feel and flow.

'In general I just try to change the question slightly – always bearing in mind that it is easy to get carried away and make it too difficult, or to play safe and make it too easy.

'People are rarely prepared to commit themselves to commenting on how good or bad your course may be until after it has been ridden. If you have made a mistake then that is too late. Unfortunately it is not possible to have a "dress rehearsal" in this game, which is why you have to be very confident about what you are doing!'

BRAMHAM AND BLENHEIM

'To compete at three-star level, a part of the qualification is to have completed an Advanced one-day event, although personally I like to have had three successful rides round Advanced tracks on any horse before I compete with it at three-star level. Compared to an Intermediate one-day track, the course is much bigger and more demanding, which is why you need to be confident at Advanced level before tackling either Blenheim or Bramham.

'Although Bramham and Blenheim offer different types of course, to my mind a horse that is capable of completing one of these tracks should also be capable of completing the other. Blenheim has a greater ratio of technical fences than Bramham, which has more of the big, bold, attacking feel about it; at three-star level you expect to meet big imposing fences, but Blenheim probably has a greater proportion of angles, corners and arrowhead-type fences than Bramham does. However, to consider a horse ready to go on to do either Badminton or Burghley I would like to think he had successfully completed both Blenheim and Bramham. If he has, then he has experienced something of everything that he is likely to meet when he goes up to four-star level.

'Three-day event courses at all levels produce less predictable results than the one-day courses, partly because of the effects of having ridden the roads and tracks, and the steeplechase – at a three-day event the rider often finds himself sitting on a "different" horse in the start-box to the one he has known at one-day events. The steeplechase can add to the boldness of some horses, with others it sends them over the top, or leaves them thinking they can hurdle all their fences. Phase C is meant to be a recovery phase before the horses have to go across country, but as was seen at the 1994 World Championships in Holland, this is not always the case: there, the oppressive heat and humidity, plus the deep sandy going, meant that many horses were unduly stressed during this phase and did not get the chance to recover as they were meant to.

'All these factors add to the unpredictability and excitement of the three-day event.'

BRAMHAM

'The triple brush at fence 4 is typical of the big, galloping fences encountered at this level. It has a very big spread, although the gap between the second and third brush has been filled in so a horse can bank it if he makes a mistake. This is a good example of thoughtful course design. It is vital to attack this fence: it needs pace, but riders also need to be able to ride up to the base of the fence so as to minimise the spread.

'Some horses did struggle with the spread of this fence, for a number of different reasons: in the case of an inexperienced horse, he may simply not have appreciated the extent of the spread. Some riders made the mistake of allowing their horses to stand off this fence. These riders would need to make a determined effort to ride up to the base of the next fence so that their horses are not continually being overstretched, thereby damaging their confidence. If the horse keeps underestimating the fences through inexperience, then probably he ought to do another three-star event before his connections decide

whether he is capable of going on to four-star level. Some horses simply do not have the scope to deal with a fence this size; in which case the rider must consider whether it is fair to keep asking the horse to compete at this level.

▼ 'In the picture below left you see how easily a fence should be jumped at this level: it is well within this horse's scope, and if he tackled the rest of the course as easily, then he is certainly ready to go on to a four-star event.

'In the second sequence Karen Dixon proves the ▶ exception to the rule! She has asked her horse to ▼ stand off this fence and so he has had to throw a huge jump – but he still looks happy and confident about it. You can see from the first picture that there is no doubt or hesitation in the rider's mind: she has decided she is going for a long stride and she makes sure the horse gets the message and picks up when she asks. Karen has never lacked grit and determination, and although some horses would not be able to cope with what she is asking here, she presumably knows this horse well enough, and he trusts her sufficiently to respond positively. Once a rider has committed himself to going on a long stride at a fence as big as this, he has to see it through – he cannot panic and check the horse at the last minute, as it would end up being buried in the bottom of the fence and unable to organise itself quickly enough to jump it safely. So although this is not the "text book" version of how to jump a big spread fence, it is a lovely example of positive, determined riding on a horse that is capable of rising to the challenge.

'The coffin at Bramham is where accuracy and technicality are both brought into the course; the rails in are big and imposing anyway, but the quickest route means riding the narrow arm of the rails, and then after the ditch, which is big, the direct route out is over a narrow logpile. In terms of dimensions and difficulty this is almost a four-star fence; moreover the ground drops away quite sharply from the rails. This is where Bramham's undulating ground provides opportunities to create interesting fences such as this.

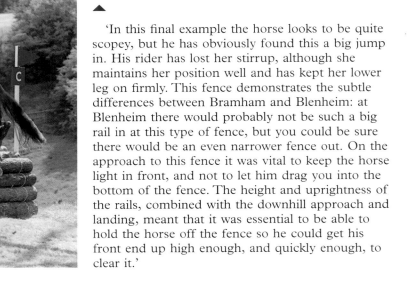

▲

'In this final example the horse looks to be quite scopey, but he has obviously found this a big jump in. His rider has lost her stirrup, although she maintains her position well and has kept her lower leg on firmly. This fence demonstrates the subtle differences between Bramham and Blenheim: at Blenheim there would probably not be such a big rail in at this type of fence, but you could be sure there would be an even narrower fence out. On the approach to this fence it was vital to keep the horse light in front, and not to let him drag you into the bottom of the fence. The height and uprightness of the rails, combined with the downhill approach and landing, meant that it was essential to be able to hold the horse off the fence so he could get his front end up high enough, and quickly enough, to clear it.'

BLENHEIM

'At Blenheim, the rider was being tested for accuracy as early as fence 4, when faced with a very technical combination compared with the triple brush that Bramham offered at the same stage in the course. The Avus fence consisted of two uprights set at right angles to each other, where to go straight through meant jumping at a very sharp angle across both elements. The longer route, as shown here, involved jumping the first element straight, and then circling round a bush to jump straight out over the second part. Jumping the direct route meant taking a calculated risk very early in the course; though if you had done this sort of exercise with your horse at home then you would have some idea as to whether he would tackle the fences at this steep an angle, or whether he would run out. At Bramham at the same stage in the course there was no choice about which route to take, and competitors just had to get on and attack the fence as there was only one way through. This combination, however, was more a test of how much homework competitors had done with their horses. But both questions needed to be asked of a potential four-star horse.

▼

'I rode The Magnate at Blenheim, and as I had practised angled fences at home, I was confident he would cope with the direct route at the Avus fence. On the day he was very good to me, because in the direct route there was only one stride between the two elements and he found this distance very long – he had to put down again and chip in a small stride. I had ridden him round Bramham in the spring, and at that stage he would not have been ready to tackle a question as technical as this. But this was three months later, and when I walked the course here at Blenheim I had been confident that he would do it for me. We had gained a lot more

experience together, and having practised jumping fences at an angle at home, I was sure that he would trust me sufficiently to do it. Besides, I wanted to get him to a four-star event the following year, and so it was important that I asked this question of him. And sure enough, the result confirmed how much more confidence the horse now had in himself and in his rider. He went where he was asked to go, and kept the line I asked for, and when it didn't go quite to plan, he was sufficiently confident to find a way out himself. Had we not practised this at home I don't imagine he would have kept going, as he wouldn't have realised what was expected of him. This just goes to show how much competition experience, and particularly relevant schooling at home, can improve a horse.

'Towards the end of the course was a double of curved palisades, each with a big ditch in front of it; the direct route meant jumping the end part of each fence which was narrow, making this an arrowhead-type question. Horse and rider are still being tested on the standard of training they have

achieved and the amount of schooling they have put in at home, and particularly on accuracy, but they are now also faced with two very big fences. Because of their size it was essential to ride forwards and attack them, but it was also vital to be able to hold a line at this speed, too. At this stage in a three-day event the horse is bound to be getting tired and a bit strung out, so riders really had to make a determined effort to gather everything together so as to have enough impulsion to take them through the combination.

'In the first sequence of photographs the horse is moving up nicely to the fence. The rider is sitting in behind him and is allowing him to open up his stride on the approach, and they have a good jump in. The horse has jumped off slightly to the right, but the rider is taking action in the air to straighten him so that they land in the right direction to ride forwards again to the second element. When we walked this combination the distance between the fences measured a very long three strides, but horses seemed to make the distance easily to meet the second palisade well.

'Compared with the first horse, the second one is not moving freely forwards to the fence; he has collected himself up and has elevated his front end, but his rider is still holding him together with a very strong contact – to my mind, once you are this close to this sort of fence you really want to be moving more positively forwards again. The horse appears to have hesitated on take-off, and as can be clearly seen in the second picture, he still has a great deal of height and spread to make up from almost a standing start. He lands a bit flat-footed, and the rider really has to work hard to try to move him up to the second element, where he does stop. It does look as if he could have jumped from where he was, but as we have said before, if you have an awkward jump over the first element of a combination, and within a few strides the horse finds himself faced with an identical fence, he has to be very brave to still want to take it on.

'I enjoy riding at both Bramham and Blenheim. Both courses have their very big fences and their technical fences, but they come in a different order

and a different ratio; so your approach to the beginning of each course is bound to be different. At Bramham it is probably easier to settle down into a rhythm and attack the course early on because the first few fences are big and imposing, they do not have an alternative, and they just need positive riding. At Blenheim, more technical questions are asked at an earlier stage, and therefore choices have to be made early on; if you decide not to tackle the direct routes, then right from the start you are having to interrupt your horse's rhythm to take the long routes. Therefore at Bramham riders must be aware of how important it is to get the horse back together and sufficiently collected to cope with the technical fences when these do occur; and at Blenheim they must be sure to let the horse open up his stride and to ride him forwards to the bigger fences when appropriate.

'Even if a horse is more suited to one of these courses than the other, I still maintain that both horse and rider should be able to cope with both before they consider competing at a four-star event.'

Riding the Over-Bold Horse

'Sidney's King is a good example of a very bold horse across country; he always wants to take his rider into his fences, and nothing at all will make him back off – he is just keen to keep going. With a horse like this it is important to try and ride him quite deep to his fences; this makes him think, and he then has to really use himself in order to get his front end up and clear of the fence. Allow him to keep standing off his fences and he will just get quicker and quicker, and more and more reckless. If a horse is inclined to do this, I would use some cross-country rounds purely as schooling exercises, keeping him in a steadier rhythm and not worrying about trying to get the time. Similarly, when jumping combination fences I keep things calm: I let him jump in, and for a four-stride distance, say, I would just sit quietly with my lower leg on and allow the four strides to develop.

'Sid has competed in two three-day events, at Bramham and Blenheim, and before each of these I used his last few cross-country outings to school him round a course slowly. Basically the horse must learn to wait and to listen to his rider, and if he is made to do this at

a couple of less important events, then he is more likely to be compliant at the three-day event when you *do* want to be riding competitively to be placed. If he has always been allowed just to run on on his own terms, then he is going to be some mean machine once he has been fired up by the steeplechase! With Sid I would set off out of the start box a little more quietly than I would normally; once he was settled in a rhythm, I would then allow him to move up a gear.

'A horse like this can be one of the most exciting and thrilling to take across country, but his rider must always be aware that his very boldness may run him into trouble. The horse doesn't realise this, and so it is up to his jockey to educate and contain him where appropriate.'

Riding the Careful Horse

'Welton Envoy – Eddy – is a horse I rate very highly, but he is far more careful and cautious than, say, Sid. However, he improves with every outing simply because his confidence and trust in his rider and in his job is increasing all the time, and this slow but steady progression is the way to produce a horse like this. It would be sensible to keep him in Novice and Intermediate classes for longer, giving him every opportunity to gain experience at a level which he won't find difficult. At this relatively early stage Eddy's natural instinct is to back himself off his fences so that he can assess and organise himself for what is coming up, and this sort of animal may at first seem harder to ride than a bold character like Sid; but in the long term an Eddy will be the better horse. Generally I have to maintain a stronger contact and a stronger lower leg with Eddy, to encourage him to take the contact forwards. He actually needs more riding into his fences, and to make the distance through combinations, than either Sid or Booze. Eddy is harder to ride because you cannot take liberties with him whilst his confidence is in the process of being built up; it is important to place him at his fences, because it would worry him if sometimes he was asked to stand off a fence, and at the next was dropped right in its base.

'Eddy has learnt a lot this season, and went round the Gatcombe Intermediate course as boldly as any horse. Now that he is really beginning to understand his work I do occasionally ask him to stand off at an easy, forgiving type of fence, just to show him that he does have the scope to jump like that when needs be.

'Galloping behind other horses at home can help this sort of character a great deal, as it encourages him to run into the bridle and to take on his rider a bit more strongly. Hunting can also work wonders. But the first priority for his rider must be *never* to scare him as he comes up through the grades: don't be afraid to use some of the alternatives on a course, so as to avoid asking too much of him each time he goes out. Be satisfied with achieving just some of the direct routes on each occasion, but even then don't overdo it because he will undoubtedly come out a braver horse the next time if he is welllooked after while he is still learning.'

The combination at Shamley Green which seemed to most impress competitors involved a palisade arrowhead, followed by a one-stride distance to the top of a natural bank, one stride down the bank, and then a stride in the bottom to a big, filled-in corner. This was a new fence on the Advanced track and was the only fence that anyone was talking about! Leslie also gave it some thought:

'My first impression when walking the course was that this was something really different. The alternative was sufficiently long that tackling the direct route was the only realistic option if you had a placing in mind. The arrowhead in was very fair, although the horse needed to be kept straight and balanced because it was a downhill approach. You knew the horse had only one stride from the arrowhead to the top of the bank, and the real problem was knowing what your horse would do then – would he jump off the top of the bank, would he just pop down it in one stride, or would he look at what lay ahead and perhaps break into trot? Whatever happened, once you were at the bottom of the bank you again had only one stride to the big corner, and here there was no room for error.

'For a combination like this, which required accuracy, it was vital to be able to keep the horse between hand and leg, and to stay behind the movement so that you could really ride the one stride to the corner. I was riding Haig, and this was his first outing since Bramham three-day event. He

is a very bold, scopey horse, but my worry was that he might just run out at the corner – being very big and long-striding, when faced with a narrow fence in a combination which comes up on him very quickly he has, in the past, occasionally run out. I was fairly confident that he would just flow through the combination taking the bank in his stride, but I knew I would have to keep my weight back and

keep him between hand and leg to ensure that he stayed straight for the corner.

'The fence needed to be approached in a bouncy, slightly-stronger-than-showjumping canter, and the horse would have to be put into this pace about ten strides out, particularly as the approach was downhill, the arrowhead was in the middle of the field, and the horse would not be fully aware of the second element until he was taking off over the first. So a controlled pace was needed to keep the horse straight and balanced, but it was also imperative to maintain the impulsion to prevent him from backing off the first element too much, and to ensure the canter had enough energy to carry him through the combination.

'As the pictures show, everything went as I had planned, even if I have got a little bit too far forwards coming in over the arrowhead; on landing I have kept my weight back, though, and have managed to stay in behind Haig as he progressed through the combination. Ideally it would have been nice to have been a little more stylish over the corner! However, my concern that he might possibly run out meant that I really had to keep hold of him until he actually took off over the fence. I was lucky to be riding a horse who took the fence on as I had planned it to be ridden, although much of that comes down to knowing your horse well enough.'

The second sequence of pictures shows Alex Munro riding a much smaller horse through the same combination. He maintains a good position coming in over the arrowhead, but his horse hesitates slightly at the top of the bank so he is pushed in front of the movement. Either it was spooked by the sand on the face of the bank, or it was looking at the second element of the combination – for whatever reason, it has fiddled in two strides down the bank; nevertheless Alex has

managed to regain his position quickly and is able to sit down and really ride for the last stride to the corner. His horse has had to reach a bit to make the spread, but Alex has kept a very good position and has given the horse the freedom it needs to stretch out over the fence.

▼

◀ The final sequence shows Jamaican rider Samantha Majendi: horse and rider have jumped in well over the arrowhead but unlike the other two competitors, Samantha has allowed her horse to trot down the bank – he may have broken into trot himself when he saw the bank, or she may have checked him to stop him leaping off it too exuberantly. However, the trot is forward-going and active, and the horse has stayed in front of the rider's leg so she has little to fear; at the bottom of the bank she has sat down and ridden for the one canter stride to the corner, which they clear easily.

As these three examples show, the most important requirement in this particular sequence of problems was to keep the horse between hand and leg no matter what it decided to do coming down the bank.

THE WATER COMPLEX

Competitors were required to jump over a table
fence which was set nearly 23ft (7m) from a set of
rails and drop into the water; there was a step out
of the water, followed by one stride to another set
of rails. 'As I walked this part of the course, the
approach to the complex felt very inviting as you
came down through a cutting in the woods to the
table. But, having walked the distance from the
table to the rails into the water, it became clear that
as the horse was going to be jumping into water, it
was quite likely that he might start to back off as he
landed over the table, so you did not know whether
he would end up taking one good stride before
jumping the rails or whether he would fiddle in a
second stride and have to clamber over the rails into
the water, with the risk of his hind legs getting
hooked up on the rails. Once you were in the water
you needed to keep the horse between hand and leg
and sitting still, allowing the horse to judge when to
make the jump up the step.

'My first ride, The Magnate, is an Advanced
horse and I was confident that he would pick up off
one stride and jump into the water. But to be sure
of this happening I knew I would have to ride
forwards to the table from about four strides out so
that he would land over the table with enough
impulsion to take one good stride followed by a
clean jump into the water. In the photo, you can see
from the horse's expression, and the way he is
carrying his head and neck, that he is coming into
the fence on an attacking stride. I have sat down to
ride him forwards to the table, and softened my
hands so that he can use his head and neck to make
a good jump. He jumps boldly over the table and
the two of us are focussed on the second element.

'I am then really riding for the one stride, and
have my stick ready to give the horse a tap on the
shoulder to ask him to pick up and take off over the
rails into the water – having committed him to
opening up his stride it would have proved very
uncomfortable for both of us if he had tried to chip
in a second stride at this stage. It is important in
this sort of situation that the rider keeps his
bodyweight back behind the movement in case this
is what the horse does. But all goes to plan and The
Magnate picks up and produces a lovely clean jump
into the water. Once in the water I am trying to
drive the horse up into my hand so that he has
sufficient balance and impulsion to jump positively
out of the water. It is difficult to "see a stride" in
water, and it is usually better to let the horse decide
when to take off, than to ride for a stride and miss,
as this will land the horse in even more trouble.'

The two photographs at the bottom of the page show Mark Corbett riding a possibly less experienced horse through the same combination. Although the horse makes a clean jump over the table and is concentrating on the next element, it has screwed its front legs slightly to the left, which shows that perhaps the combination has taken it a little by surprise. It then starts to veer to the left which actually increases the distance to the second element, and from Mark's expression and position it is clear he has anticipated that the horse is going to pop in a second stride. In jumping it then leaves a front leg behind, a common occurrence when a horse is faced with a drop or water, and Mark is having almost to lift it over the obstacle. The horse's expression throughout the sequence shows that it is very genuine but just a little surprised – and despite having a rather uncomfortable jump into the water, he is concentrating on the next challenge.

Leslie also rode Brownshill Boy round the same track: 'Brownshill Boy is an even more attacking horse than The Magnate. He picked up easily on one stride, and with him, I really had no option but to ride for one stride as he is such a bold, confident horse – I would have got us both into all kinds of trouble if I had tried to hold him up for two strides. With The Magnate, although I rode for one stride, I was well aware of the fact that he might just have hesitated once he landed over the table, and he could have chipped in a second stride. In this sort of instance it is important that, as a rider, you commit yourself to one option or the other, and nine times out of ten, if you know your horse well enough, it will work. And provided you keep your weight back behind the movement and do not attack the combination with excessive speed but with plenty of impulsion, you and the horse will also cope if he should tackle the fence other than the way you had planned.'

Listening to Leslie describe his ride round the course at Gatcombe leaves you feeling as if you have just survived a rollercoaster ride: the layout of the fences and the natural terrain mean that riders are constantly chasing uphill, swinging round and flying downhill, back up, round and down again. But if it is exhausting having the course described to you, then imagine what it demands of the horse and rider tackling it for real!

Leslie had two rides at Gatcombe: Lowenac had qualified for the Intermediate Championship, and The Magnate was running in one of the Advanced sections. Both horses followed the same track, a slightly shortened version of the British Open Championship course.

'The fences at Gatcombe are not huge,' says Leslie, 'but the terrain, which alters very quickly, is extremely influential. Gatcombe doesn't allow you to get away with any lapse of concentration at all. At most events you can afford to use the first few fences to settle yourself and the horse into a nice rhythm before having too much else to worry about, but Gatcombe doesn't afford that luxury; the first two fences are straightforward, but they need to be jumped well and with great determination, because the third fence is a very serious one! Because of this, at Gatcombe I always programme my mind to think of the practice fence as the first three or four fences on the course and so ask the horse to jump it more than I would normally, using it to settle us into a nice rhythm and to get his full attention. So when we leave the start box we are both mentally prepared for the questions that come up immediately.

'I rode The Magnate first, and having made good use of the practice fence in getting us settled and concentrating, rode out of the start box trying to pick up our rhythm as quickly as possible. At fence 2 I took a stronger contact to push him up between hand and leg more than I would normally at such a straightforward jump; I wanted him collected and working in a much shorter frame than usual so that I had sufficient control and impulsion for fence 3. This is a sizeable log, sited off a turn, and at the top of a very steep wooded bank. I used the turn to ask for even more engagement, then concentrated on holding the horse with that same impulsion and engagement all the way to the fence. It was important to feel the horse jumping into the hand with each stride, but not running through it – the aim is to give the horse just enough time to see

where he is going, but not so much that he might think about stopping. At this fence a rider can't afford to worry about the steepness of the landing; in riding the approach, pretend that it is flat, and only once the horse has definitely taken off can you afford to slip the reins and sit back to allow for the steep descent. Let the horse find his own feet, and don't rush him on the loose shale which covers the bank. Once on the level and approaching the next fence, an ascending oxer, it is possible to take up more contact and push the horse up into the hand again.

'Once out of the woods the course heads towards the Landrover Folly. This really represents no more than a serious grid exercise, except the jumps won't fall down: a big parallel followed by five strides to another parallel, then one stride to an arrowhead.

The two parallels were not in a straight line, and competitors had to ride a so-called "dog-leg". Because of this there was some leeway in the distance, and it was possible to ride either for five or six strides – the decision had to be based on how well a rider knew his horse. This fence proved to be particularly influential throughout the event, and I decided to ride the longer alternative here. The Magnate is not very experienced and I felt his nerve might already have been a little rattled coming down over fence 3 and the steep descent that followed.'

To tackle the direct route successfully at the Landrover Folly the first priority was to get the horse off his forehand, having just run down such a steep bank; so a rider needed to come out of the woods and use half-halts to engage the back end so that the forehand became lighter. In this sequence having made a good jump over the first parallel, everything looked in order; the rider was in a good position, and the horse was engaged and off his forehand. But then problems creep in, the horse has thrown his head up and looks to be resisting: perhaps he was being held too strongly so that when the rider came to steer him through the dog-leg he objected by fighting the rider's hand and hollowing out. At the second parallel the horse jumps slightly off to the right; the rider has tried to pull him back on course but he has found an excuse to run out. They had actually landed very steeply over the parallel and the horse was very much on his forehand, and this would have made it difficult for him to focus on the arrowhead and to organise himself quickly enough to tackle it successfully.

This fence requires such accuracy that you just cannot get away with this kind of problem: the horse has to be balanced and also soft and round. This rider has probably had to use too much hand, thus causing the horse to hollow; consequently its attention was on the rider rather than on the fence in front.

The next picture sequence shows a different horse and rider: the same degree of collection and engagement is shown as by the first horse, but having jumped the first parallel this one is still soft, attentive, and totally focussed on the second parallel. They meet this well, and as the horse is landing you can see he has kept his head and neck up and is already focussed on the arrowhead – and so he makes nothing of this combination.

'Leslie continues with his account of his ride with The Magnate: 'As you left this combination it was the first chance there was to allow the horse to gallop on a bit, so I let The Magnate power on towards the Breitling Watchstrap (below right). This involved a step up, followed by a short stride to the Watchstrap, which was very bright and very upright. As we came up the bank towards the step I just eased off the pace a bit; the gradient of the hill is sufficient to slow the horse up, so you could have him quite short and collected by the time you got to the step without too much effort. The shape of the Watchstrap meant that you needed good control to ensure the horse didn't glance away from the watch-face and actually run out: by using the gradient of the hill rather than your hand to steady and balance the horse you avoided the risk of losing too much impulsion. The step itself further helped to back the horse off the very upright fence; you just needed to hold the horse between hand and leg so that he stayed straight.

'From here you ran on to a straightforward stone wall. I allowed the horse just to run on to this fence but kept a nice contact to support and balance him as there is a decent drop the other side. On landing I picked him up very quickly to balance him before making the turn towards the steps, using the turn to help create more engagement and impulsion. It was important to act quickly to lighten the forehand, as coming over a drop fence tends to throw the horse onto his front end. It was a bounce up the first step, then a short stride to the second step, followed by a bounce up the third. This required a great deal of effort, but at the same time it was very important to contain the power you had created – if you didn't, the horse might jump too far up onto the second step and then he wouldn't be able to manage either a bounce or a stride. A very scopey horse might bounce all the way up, but I wasn't riding a horse like that. As I expected, The Magnate felt a little bit blown at the top of the steps, not unusual at this stage in the course and following such a jumping effort; so I allowed him two or three strides to recover his breath before re-establishing the rhythm and the pace we had had before.

'We galloped on to a straightforward ditch and hedge which I took at a slight angle to make the turn towards the next fence easier; doing this allows you to save time without sapping the horse's energy reserves. After this let-up fence there is then a long gallop across the top of the park by the car parks before you come to the hayrack. I just balanced him on the turn to this and eased off the pace a little, and let him take it in his stride; we then ran down the bank to the barn complex.

'I was a little apprehensive about tackling this on this particular horse. There was an extremely upright gate before the barn, and The Magnate does have a tendency occasionally to leave a front leg behind over very upright fences. Before the turn I collected him up and rode at the gate in a really

short, sharp canter as if I was in the showjumping ring; but my worst fears were realised when he still managed to hit it really hard with his front leg. It was very frustrating as I felt I had done everything I could to help him, and he just didn't respond. Looking back, I wonder if it happened *because* I rode with that in mind; but it is hard to ignore such a possibility when you know the horse well enough to anticipate what he is likely to do. At the time, however, everything was happening too quickly to dwell on it, as the next fence was only three strides away! This was the palisade into the barn, followed by four strides to a big hayrack on the way out. Despite hitting the gate very hard we did stay together, probably because we had approached the fence in balance and in control; I quickly took hold

of the horse and used my hands, legs and seat to pick him up and ride forwards to the palisade, and on again to the hayrack – the hayrack has to be attacked as it is a big fence, and he did jump it well.

'After this combination you have to turn very quickly to a wall and a drop off the lane, so as soon as we were in the air over the hayrack I focussed my attention on the wall as this helps you make the turn in time. As we landed and started the turn I pushed him up to the contact to lighten the forehand and to create a bouncy rhythm down to the drop wall. This is followed by another sharp turn, as the ropes marking the course here take a very tight line. I let the horse land and take one stride before asking for the turn; if you try to turn as you land he can slip up.

'From here on I was working to keep the horse light in front, and concentrating hard as the next question was a double of corners. The course ran down a steep bank, and at the bottom turned through 90° to line up for the corners which were set on two strides. Before I started the turn I fixed my eye on the first corner; doing this helps you come out of the turn at the right time so as to give you the line and distance you want – and I used the turn to help lighten the horse's forehand and really get his hocks engaged. Then it is all about keeping the horse straight and between hand and leg, and keeping your eye on the first and then the second corner.

'In the next sequence of pictures I am taking the corners on my less experienced ride, Lowenac. The turn helps you collect the horse and lighten the forehand. As I approach the first corner the horse is obviously focussed on the fence; he jumps it well and as he lands his attention is on the second element. My lower leg has come a little too far forwards and in fact I have just lost the horse's outside shoulder, which could have allowed him to run out. Realising this I have tried to push him forwards and straight, which has left me a little bit behind him on the approach; to compensate I have then thrown myself too far forwards up his neck on take-off – there is too much daylight between myself and the saddle. However, in the air over the corner we seem to have regained our composure and everything looks correct and organised again. The emphasis at this fence, as at most of Captain Mark Phillips' combinations, is on being able to ride a straight line.

'Next came another upright stone wall; The Magnate was beginning to run on a little bit free down the slight descent to the wall, so I did check him back a bit – though I would have preferred not to have done this, but just allowed him to jump out of his stride. He is a horse I have always had difficulty in getting to do this as he seems to like being set up for his fences; but it would help his self-confidence if sometimes he put his trust in the two of us and just took them as they came. However, there followed an Aintree-type fence, and because it was so straightforward I concentrated on leaving him alone and just riding forwards towards it. If he was forced to take it in his stride I hoped it would increase his confidence in himself and me, but if he didn't like it then I felt because it was an easy enough fence we would get away with it – I wanted him to learn to think for himself, and not to rely on me. As we approached the fence I could feel him start to think "Come on Dad, do something!"

and he was obviously quite shocked that I continued to do nothing, and so he jumped the fence a little bit free; but as he galloped away I sensed that he had at last just realised that he *could* manage things on his own – and his jumping became more confident as we continued. We ran on over undulating ground to the parallel rail and he jumped this extremely well and with great composure, almost as if he was showing off his new sense of achievement.

'We were now back in the heart of the park and heading down the hill to a log trakehner. It wasn't a very big fence, but the downhill approach meant you were looking straight into the ditch – I never had a good feel from the horse either on the approach to this fence, or in the way he jumped it, and it wasn't made any easier because he was landing into rising ground, which is never pleasant for a horse. Of all the fences in the Intermediate Championship this is the one I would like to see

taken out as it gave you no feeling at all – you just jumped into the bank the other side and it stopped you dead. The Advanced horses are more experienced and generally more resilient, and have had to cope with this sort of thing before, but for the younger horses, like Lowenac, in the Intermediate Championship it was very discouraging.

'Having landed over the trakehner I gave the horse a couple of strides to recover and pick himself up from the horrible landing before asking for more impulsion and acceleration as we went away round the turn to the silver birch rails before the water. When the approach to a fence is off a turn like this you use it to increase the engagement and impulsion on the approach; then keep the horse light in front and going forwards in a coffin-type canter. Once we had landed over the rails I just kept him between hand and leg and let him run on in his stride to the water. I sat deep into the saddle on the

last three strides and made sure I stayed behind him; it was a big drop into the water, so I slipped the reins and sat well back to allow for this. I picked him up after the first stride in the water and then sat behind him, keeping him jumping into my hand with that extra bit of "oomph" which you need to counteract the drag from the water.'

All the way down the hill to the silver birch rails and the water, the rider needed to be working to lighten the forehand and balance the horse; he will also have to be careful that it doesn't get carried away by the momentum created by the hill. It is as well to adopt a safety position over the rails, with the lower leg further forward and the shoulders slightly further back than usual, so as to be in a position to help, rather than hinder the horse should he hit the fence or peck on landing. But if a rider can balance his horse and just help it off the floor with his hand, then the back end usually follows safely.

keep her weight back behind the horse. The last photo shows clearly just how much spray can be produced and why it is important for the rider to be sitting back because of the drag from the water. It is usually in the stride after landing that the effects of the spray are at their worst, and when the horse needs encouragement and support to find his way through. Having survived the jump in *and* the effects of the spray, horse and rider then need to focus on the exit rails, and the rider must always work to keep everything going forwards – you have to overemphasise everything to make sure the horse has enough impulsion and balance, without actually rushing him, to jump rails such as this out of water successfully.

▲

Once over the birch rails the course is still running downhill, so you must keep working to lighten the front end as the next question is another big fence, and into water; however, it is a related distance so as long as a rider picks himself and the horse up straightaway after landing, he should meet it well. It is important to drop into the saddle and ride the horse forwards for the last three strides so that it doesn't have a chance to stop or take too much of a look. In the sequence of photos the rider is sitting up and sending the horse forwards; she then obviously senses that the horse might back off, and has picked up her stick to reinforce the message – although her arm has been thrown back as they start to land over the fence (commonly known as 'hailing a cab'), this has actually helped

Leslie continues with his account of the Gatcombe course: 'You then turned to a narrow trakehner-type fence where it was essential to have the horse absolutely straight; so as soon as we had left the water complex safely behind us I picked the horse up again, got him round the turn and then concentrated on getting his shoulders really straight for the approach to the trakehner. Once I knew I had him straight and focussed on the fence I rode him strongly forwards towards it.'

In the picture sequence the rider has taken a strong contact and has ridden the horse up into his hand and both are focussed on the fence. He rides forwards to it, meets it on a good distance, and the horse throws a lovely jump.

'At this point in the course my thoughts were that we were still clear, we didn't have much more to tackle, and that if we could get home safely we would have a good chance of being placed. I felt we had been making quite good time over the course, and opted to take the long route at the narrow arrowhead fence which followed; it was the only real risk left on the course.'

Here, Mary Thomson and King Boris make it look easy; although the previous year Mary was amongst several riders who lost their chance of glory here: it is quite a decent ditch for such a narrow fence and it is tempting to the horse just to glance off to either side. At this sort of question it is important to have the horse straight and focussed, and to know that you will meet it on a good distance so that you can ride forwards with impulsion and a strong contact, keeping behind the horse ready to correct even the slightest deviation.

Leslie continues: 'Now we had a line of straightforward fences left – but at this point the horse will be starting to feel pretty leg-weary. So my priority was to encourage the horse forwards again, to get him motivated and moving away from my leg, and just to keep running as it is an uphill climb to the last two fences. These are straightforward but big, and a tired horse needs help from its rider. The Magnate felt better than he might have done at this point but I just kept niggling at him to keep going; on a tired horse it is essential that you support him with a good contact but keep the leg on to encourage and motivate him; it also keeps his mind on you and the job in hand, and prevents him

The British Open Championship

The horses in the Open Championship class at Gatcombe jump some additional and more demanding fences than those doing the Advanced sections.

Having jumped the double of corners and the big parallel rails which brought competitors back into the main bowl of the park, the championship horses then tackled a big parallel of hedges in the bottom of the bowl. The steepness of the slope on the approach to this fence often causes horses to 'prop', and makes what would normally be a straightforward big fence a *very* big fence because of the terrain. At this sort of fence a rider would normally be able to use pace to his advantage, by opening the horse up a little and riding it forwards to the fence, letting it take it in its stride – but at Gatcombe the downhill slope does not allow you to do this. Thus on approaching the bottom of the hill a rider must really close his legs around the horse and give it as much help as he can, because the poor approach will make this a very big effort indeed.

In the photo the fence is being ridden by an experienced rider, Bruce Davidson, but even his horse is having to stretch to make the spread. (The fence had been made safe as the middle had been filled in, so horses could touch down on top if they had to.)

Next came a corner at the top of a very steep bank. As with any corner, the horse required setting up, but equally important was the need to make sure the back end was really engaged, and that no impulsion had been lost on the approach; here again the uphill approach can be used to help set the horse up rather than the rider using too much hand to do the same job. Once the horse is balanced and on the correct line, he must be able to accelerate forwards to the fence; there is no flat ground to take off from, so again it makes this a big jump. Finding a good take-off distance at a fence like this is not as important as making sure the horse has enough impulsion – once he reaches the lip of the bank he will usually take off as long as he has sufficient impulsion.

switching his thoughts to his tiredness.

'The Magnate finished with a good time to take eighth place. Lowenac had spoilt his chances in the showjumping where he had had three down, so although he was clear across country I had only taken him quietly. The Magnate in particular came away from this event feeling much more confident in himself, and it was noticeable even in his day-to-day behaviour at home. If a horse can finish an event feeling he has achieved something, then he will find the next event that little bit easier. If you can keep building on this, then you are on the way to producing a good horse.'

▲
In the next sequence Matt Ryan takes the fence in exemplary fashion: first he just checks his horse to get its concentration, but without losing the power from the back end or the rhythm. The horse arrives on the top of the bank with good impulsion, and Matt has kept his own position well, particularly the strong lower leg which helps fire the horse off the ground. He would then release his arms and hands forwards to allow the horse the freedom to use itself over the fence.

Having run up the hill the horses are often a bit leg-weary, and it is important that riders allow them a few strides to regain their composure; the next combination involves a lot of things happening very quickly, so both horse and rider need a few seconds to gather thoughts and energy for the challenge. The course drops back down the hill, over a palisade, followed by a big drop and then an arrowhead palisade. It is important to collect the horse very much between hand and leg, with his hocks

well underneath him, otherwise the momentum of the downhill run will throw him onto his forehand; and the first palisade demands attacking riding as it is big enough to cause a stop if you are half-hearted. It also needs to be ridden with contained power, because on landing the horse must be able to pull himself up and just pop off the drop, and not go careering off down the hill.

The next series of photos shows a rider who has 'showjumped' the first palisade and got a nice jump over it; he has slipped the reins sufficiently but has retained the contact so that he can contain and balance the horse before the next element. He has also kept his weight behind the horse so that when it is faced with the drop, he is in a good position to encourage it off the edge – and it *is* a big drop, so he needs to slip the reins. However, he must still keep the contact because of the third element, and this rider is in the ideal position to just guide and balance the horse – gravity takes over here because of the momentum gathered from the slope, and he just wants to lightly guide the horse but without interfering with him. It would not be advisable really to take hold of the horse's head here, because he would probably resist by throwing his head up or down, and would lose his balance and his focus on the next fence. The rider has to concentrate on keeping his own balance, and his line; so it is important to look up! Finally the horse picks up and jumps the arrowhead. In this situation there is no time to shorten the reins as the horse starts to elevate his front end, so the rider has to draw his elbow and hand back in order to maintain the contact, thus preventing the horse from running out.

The next photographs show how easily things can go wrong: this horse has jumped the first palisade with great exuberance, and having launched himself over the fence he has succeeded in leaving his rider behind him somewhat. She has then had to keep a hold of the horse to make sure that they have sufficient control for the drop that follows, so it is not quite such a happy-looking picture: they have got to the edge of the drop before they have had time to rebalance themselves. The horse has bulged out through the left shoulder before coming off the drop, and on landing has overreacted to his rider's efforts to straighten him up and has started to run to the right; so he has had to be hauled back on line to meet the arrowhead successfully. In all fairness the rider has got the job done, but luck was perhaps on her side.

In this sort of combination, therefore, the emphasis is on getting a controlled and balanced approach and jump over the first element, and then just staying behind the horse, maintaining a contact and keeping the lower leg on, and guiding him through the rest. The championship course then ran on down to the water, from where was the same as the Advanced.

Captain Mark Phillips CVO

GATCOMBE & BURGHLEY

Captain Mark Phillips retired from an illustrious eventing career – which included winning Badminton four times, winning Burghley in 1973, riding in the Gold medal winning team at the Munich Olympics, Team Gold at the 1970 World Championships, Team Silver in 1974, and Team Gold at the 1971 European Championships – to concentrate on training event riders at home and abroad, and on course designing. He is the American team trainer, course advisor to the American Horse Shows Association and course designer for both the British Open at Gatcombe and for the Burghley three-day event.

'As a rough rule of thumb every course should have a beginning, a middle and an end, with most of the "questions" coming in the middle section. At a three-day event it is particularly important to ensure the last section of the course is not too arduous as the horses could be tiring. At a one-day event there is more margin for adjustment as the horses should not be tired at the end of the course. The terrain can upset your plans; at Gatcombe, fence 3 poses a difficult question very early in the course, but I have to get the riders down through that steep section of wood somehow. The fence is relatively small and, being a log, is quite kind to both horse and rider. If this same question came later in the course the fence would most certainly be bigger, and I might not give it such quite an inviting profile.

'Generally I try to be as kind as possible to the horse in terms of the profile of the fence and the materials I use. I want to give him every chance to jump the fence. I test the rider by the positioning of the fence, and by the relation of the fences to each other. There is a very fine line between asking a question of a rider and yet still making the fence sympathetic to the horse. The materials you use play a big part in this; sawn timber and stone walls are very unforgiving, whereas brush and round timber is much kinder, and there is a whole range of possibilities in between.

'Twenty years ago we were jumping courses of big, straightforward fences; today that would not produce the required result. Now there is a tendency to split fences into two categories – the big, awe-inspiring "rider-frighteners", and technical fences – but there are many ways of playing on the

rider's mind other than by the size of the fence. One principle of course design is that anything you build with an uphill approach is relatively easy, because the hill balances the horse for the rider. Anything approached downhill puts the emphasis on the rider as he has to work hard to help the horse achieve the necessary balance from which to jump. Therefore at four-star level you would expect to find more fences with downhill approaches than you would at Novice level; you expect the rider at a four-star event to know how to deal with the problem.

'If you never make a mistake course building then you are not trying very hard; it is very easy to be conservative, but then your course will hold few fears for the majority of riders, and you run the risk of having a glorified dressage competition on your hands! You have to be bold, and you have to experiment, and yet you have to be constantly aware of the tightrope you tread; it is also easy to overdo it. Everything comes and goes in popularity, and you can suddenly find yourself overdoing one aspect of a course – I have been through a phase of building perhaps too many "narrow-type" fences – and then you have to go back to improving the balance of the course. But all the time you are trying to find something new, trying to push the barriers back a touch further, not only for the sake of interest and furthering the riders' experience, but also for the entertainment of the spectators.

'Occasionally you build a fence where a good number of the riders do not quite "twig" what you are asking of them, and then the fence does not work. A fence like this is probably ahead of its time, so the following year you have to take it back a step, before building back up to it or something similar in subsequent events. The Barbour Zip fence which I introduced some years ago to the British Open Championship was a good example of this. It was basically a step up to a bounce over a rail. But I added zig-zag rails which ran from the rail back to the step. My idea was for the riders to jump the step where it was highest, and where the zig-zag rails formed a V, in the same way as you would place centreing poles on a showjump when schooling. The idea of centreing poles is to back the horse off the fence and to make him snap his front end up cleanly. However, on the day a great number of riders jumped the step where it was lowest, and where the V was formed *towards* them; this meant their horses threw a very big jump up the step, and got too close to the rail to bounce out successfully.

'Every time you build a course you learn something new, and you learn even more when you see it ridden. I sometimes feel that riders do not appreciate how much thought goes into a lot of the fences; they don't always stop to think "Why has he asked this question here? What is he testing me on?" Every fence has a particular purpose and is designed in a certain way, and is positioned for a reason. Riders need to appreciate this when they walk the course to make sure they are attempting to answer the same questions the designer is asking

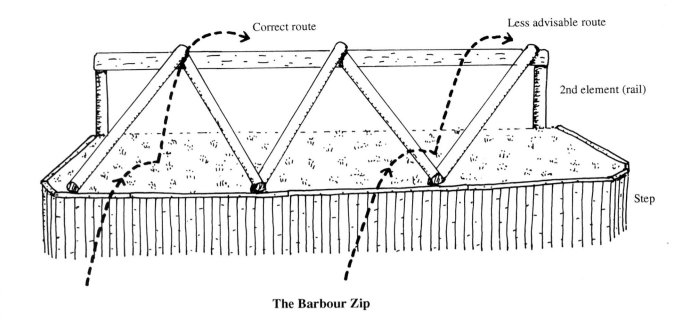

Correct route   Less advisable route

2nd element (rail)

Step

The Barbour Zip

them. This applies more at Advanced level, because at Novice level you should still be building courses which will educate both horse and rider. The higher up the scale you go the more you try to test the rider, while always trying to be fair to the horse.

'Riders also need to be more aware of how the terrain can help them ride the course; you often see a rider trying to steady his horse a long way from the fence, whereas on some occasions if he had just let him run on to it the terrain, or the design of the fence, would often back the horse off naturally. Instead, horse and rider have wasted time and energy battling with each other unnecessarily. The course designer uses the ground to ask questions of horse and rider, but the thinking rider will also use the ground to help him solve the puzzle.'

THE 1993 INTERMEDIATE CHAMPIONSHIPS

'Gatcombe hosted the Intermediate Championships for the first time in 1993. We had run an Advanced class at Gatcombe for many years before that and the class was often won by a first-time-out Advanced horse, so I thought the Intermediate Championship horses would be able to jump round the Advanced track quite happily. As it turned out, the young Advanced horses partnered by experienced riders were fine, but the course caused mayhem for those combinations of inexperienced horse *and* rider. What the championship really needed was an easy Advanced course, not a full-up Advanced track.

'The first question came at fence 3 which, as I explained earlier, is a steep piece of terrain which has to be negotiated somehow. The log was purposely set a little further back from the steep descent so that the horses had some flat ground to land on.

'The Landrover Folly at fence 5 really needed to be ridden at to make the distance in the

combination. Having come down the steep slope through the woods it was easy to forget to get the horse motoring on again and, generally, it was lack of sufficient pace and impulsion which led to problems at this fence. In 1994 I modified it to an oxer followed by five or six strides to an angled rail. After the previous year's experience I erred on the side of caution at this fence and it really was quite straightforward; I wanted the riders to feel good about the fence again.

'The Breitling Watchstrap is on a site which has been particularly difficult to build on over the years. The step is not very big, so it is easy for horses to overjump and get too close to whatever you build on the top, and there is also quite a steep run up to it so riders can find it difficult to keep the horses up and on their feet at the top. There is not enough room to build more than one fence on this site, so whatever is there has to be suitable for the Intermediate, the Advanced and the British Open Championship horses. I designed the straps of the watch to come back towards the step, as in this way they would help to back the horses off the upright fence.

'The Steps were one of the original Gatcombe fences, but caused numerous problems for the Intermediates in 1993. Four steep steps like these really needed to be attacked hard as you lose a little ground each time you jump up one. You came off a turn to the steps and the riders who had problems just failed to pick up enough pace on the approach. The following year I altered the course so that the Intermediates first jumped through a sympathetically-built road crossing – in over a small wall, then up a bank followed by a couple of strides to some bales out – before then coming *down* the steps.

'At the barn complex there is quite a nasty turn beforehand and the camber of the ground is wrong, but both these factors force the rider to collect and balance the horse. This is why I then put in an upright fence, the gate, as the horse should already be in the right balance and pace to jump such a fence. The riders can then go safely forwards to tackle the fences into and out of the barn.

'I used the double of corners in both 1993 and 1994; of all the fences I had built for the first year of the championship, this was one which I had thought would cause plenty of problems in terms of run-outs. But it rode very well which is why it survived through to the following year. Again I think the terrain helped the riders here; they came down a steep hill and had to turn into the fence. The horses tended to prop down the hill and remained balanced, rather than run on down on their forehands, which is what I had expected to happen.

'The log trakehner down in the bottom of the valley is one of those fences with a downhill approach and an uphill landing; these never really flow and the horses usually land a bit four square on the other side, but there is a natural ditch there and so we have to get over it somehow. The log is kind to the horse and the fence is really quite low, so one such question on the course is not too much to ask. I could build up the landing and take-off

areas to make them level, but I like to use the natural land features and if I did level it off I would make the fence bigger and perhaps harder.

'The water complex has been the same for several years; the silver birch rails generally jump well although horses never give them a lot of air. I used them for the first Intermediate Championship in 1933, but have since taken them out for the Intermediate horses.

'The profile of the fence going into the water is very kind, which makes up for the artificial material which forms the steel gas cylinder; because of the downhill approach I would not build a vertical fence into the water here. At this type of fence the horse should be given a chance to see where he is going so that he can lower himself into the water over the fence. In 1993 the Intermediates also had to jump the silver birch rails, and these were supposed to help set them up for the water jump. You could ride five or six strides from the rails to the water; the correct thing to do was to ride six so that the horse was in a short, bouncy canter, and could then pop over the fence into the water. If you came on five you were attacking the water with some pace and the result was a few unseated riders. I think we will see related distances used more and more in cross-country courses, and if riders understand them properly, and their horses are rideable, they will tackle the problems easily. I used a related distance at Burghley from the Beehives to the Sunken Road, and that claimed a surprising victim in Ginny Elliott (Leng). She realised she needed to fit in an extra stride as she landed over the Beehives, but was unable to contain her horse sufficiently to do it; the result was too big a jump into the sunken road and a refusal when her mare found she was too close to the bank to jump out.

'From the water onwards the course stayed the same for 1993 and 1994. The few remaining questions all had options, and I felt it was at this point that we would separate those who were still riding to win from those who wanted a more cautious ride home.'

BADMINTON

There is very little difference these days between Badminton and Burghley in terms of the severity of the course; they are both big four-star three-day events, but Badminton seems to be the one that everybody wants to win. It has so much history and the atmosphere is electric, and it is this that is transmitted to the competitors. Over the years the late Frank Weldon has moulded the relatively flat terrain by introducing many different elements such as grassed-over banks, and all these have created terrific feature fences.

There are several things that make the big three-day events very different to anything else. To start with, competitors are at the event for a long time, which means it is easier for their concentration to wander – they will be thinking about the course for at least three days before they actually ride it. Then once they are on the roads and tracks their mind will be constantly thinking about the course, the condition of the horse, then whether or not the steeplechase went well – if it didn't, they will be worrying about whether they will get their act together again on the cross country. And all this before they actually have to gallop four-and-a-half miles and jump thirty fences.

Nor must the effect of the huge number of spectators ever be underestimated. The first year Leslie rode at Badminton he was warned by a more experienced competitor that on cross-country day itself, the rider's view of the course is completely altered by the vast crowds. His advice was to make sure that any markers he had chosen to use were not masked by the crowd on cross-country day, and warned him to be aware that neither horse nor rider would sight the fences as quickly because of the number of people. This is something which is especially important to remember from the horse's point of view, because he has never seen the course and he will not have a clear view of many of the fences until he comes round the last corner to them – he won't have been able to focus on the jump from, say, half a field away, which is usually the case at a one-day event. And on top of all that, the way the course rides at Badminton and Burghley always seems for some reason to be less predictable than it does at other events – the rider always sets off with a feeling that he is heading into the unknown.

Leslie was unable to ride at Badminton in 1994, but he describes how the course looked to ride.

The Speed and Endurance Phases

At a three-day event, on cross-country day, horse and rider have to tackle the roads and tracks phases, plus a steeplechase, before having a ten-minute break and then riding the cross-country course. Phase A of the roads and tracks section is meant to serve as a warm-up for the horse before he tackles the steeplechase course, Phase B. This is followed by Phase C, another section of roads and tracks, which allows the horse time to recover from the steeplechase as well as testing his fitness and endurance; towards the end of Phase C he makes his way back to the ten-minute halt box and the start of the cross-country course, Phase D. Leslie explains his procedure on speed and endurance day:

'I don't believe that Phase A alone is sufficient to warm a horse up to gallop and jump at speed on the steeplechase, so I always have mine walked around in hand for at least twenty minutes before the start of Phase A. If his start time isn't until later in the day, then he will be led

out of his stable two or three times for fifteen to twenty minutes walking in hand.

'The roads and tracks are usually covered at a speed of four minutes per kilometre, and there are kilometre markers the whole way round the route so that you can check your progress. How easy or otherwise it is to make the time depends on your horse, his length of stride and way of going, but generally you need to maintain a good working trot for most of the way.

'I like to give the horse a canter if there is a suitable stretch of ground, as this helps to warm up all the different muscles thoroughly, and it usually makes up enough time for me to then let him have a walk somewhere. I aim to arrive at the start of the steeplechase about two minutes ahead of time, as this allows me to walk the horse round so that he is as fully recovered as possible, and also to have a last minute check of his girth, shoes, boots or bandages.'

THE STEEPLECHASE
'The main aim on the steeplechase is to settle as quickly as possible into the rhythm and pace required to get round in the time. Experience is really the only way to learn what this speed is, but working out 'minute markers' and knowing where the halfway mark is will help you to judge your pace. It is essential to use a metre wheel to work out the minute markers, and there is nearly always someone at a three-day event with one of these. The halfway point is usually marked anyway.

'Successful and safe steeplechasing also comes down to experience, and as I have said before, for those wanting to improve this skill, any chance to ride work for a racehorse trainer can only be advantageous. And watch how the good National Hunt jockeys ride on the approach to a fence and over it – this is always educational.

'At this stage horses will have seen steeplechase fences on other

Ten-minute box equipment

Towels

Good selection of rugs

Some first-aid equipment, especially wound cream and powder

Cross-country grease

Buckets, sponges, scrapers: fill the buckets with water well beforehand so that it warms up to the ambient temperature

Spare watch and whip

Spare bandages, boots, tape

Spare set of shoes and studs

Stud kit

Drink for rider

---

cross-country courses, and the only difference is the speed at which they must be tackled on this phase; but the priorities are the same as they are for any jumping, that is, balance, rhythm and awareness of pace. So don't gallop flat out and then take a great pull in front of a fence, but try to keep the horse coming to each one so that he can jump out of his stride. Just elevate the upper body as you come to them, push all the weight down into the heel, and then either sit in quietly behind the horse and let him come in and pop over neatly, or press him on so he produces a good flowing jump out of his stride.

'Ideally try to finish with five to ten seconds in hand; and coming through the finish it is best to allow the gallop to wind down gradually, through canter to trot and then walk – if the horse tries to pull himself up quickly he risks straining a muscle, so it is important to keep the leg on and support him with the contact so that he does slow up gradually. By letting him trot for a few strides you can feel if he is sound, or a little jarred up from the chase.

'Competitors are allowed a helper at the stopping point, which is between the end of the steeplechase and the start of Phase C; keep going, but take the opportunity to check that your boots or bandages are all right, and the helper must check that the horse has all four shoes. If it is very hot he or she might just quickly sponge some water over the horse, or maybe hand the rider a bottle of water to pour over its neck as they go along. The helper should be armed with spare equipment for the steeplechase phase, and this should include a spare bridle, breastplate, stirrup and leather, and a girth; a spare set of shoes, with studs if worn; bandaging tape, spare bandages or boots; and finally a bucket and sponge, and a bottle of water.

PHASE C

'There is a little more time to play with on Phase C, although it is still best to aim for an average of one kilometre every four minutes. It is generally of most benefit to the horse to allow him longer to cover the first kilometre after the steeplechase, so as to help him recover as quickly as possible. So having galloped through the finish of Phase B, the steeplechase, I would gradually bring the horse back to canter, then trot and then to walk. Usually I try to give the horse six minutes to cover the first kilometre, walking him for two or three minutes and then picking up the trot again, and possibly five for the second, if time allows letting him have another little walk. When we gallop the horses at home they walk for a couple of minutes, then trot back down to the start of the gallop and run up it again, so they are used to this sort of recovery process.

'When walking the roads and tracks phases it is important to note what the going is like all the way round; sometimes there will be patches where the horses will have to walk, in which case that time will have to be made up somewhere else. At the 1994 World Championships in The Hague, the going on Phase C was very deep and loose in places so the riders had to walk for these, and then canter on over the stretches where the ground was better. A competitor must have all this in his mind, and should not just assume that he can set off and be able to trot safely the whole way round.

'At the competitors' briefing at the start of the event, you are normally told to trot the last 100 yards of Phase C so the veterinary panel can check that the horse is sound as you come into the ten-minute box. I try to get to the box about two minutes ahead of my allocated time, so that once the vet has finished checking the horse's heart and respiration rate, you still have the full ten minutes to prepare for the cross-country.'

TEN-MINUTE BOX PROCEDURE

As you enter the ten-minute box you will be asked to dismount by the vets; run up the stirrups immediately and slacken the girth and noseband while they check the horse's heart and respiration rates. If it is cold a rug should be put over the horse's hindquarters as soon as he comes into the box. The vets will usually also ask if you had a good ride on the steeplechase so that they know whether to check for any other possible problems. If they are worried about your horse's condition they will ask to check him again a few minutes later.

'As soon as this first check is finished, lead the horse over to where your helpers have made their base in the ten-minute box. You don't want too many people fussing around; have one person to put a headcollar on over the bridle and to hold him, while someone else checks the shoes and studs and then goes on to refresh the horse. Any readjustment of boots or bandages should be done now, and we also readjust the saddle at this point, undoing the girth, lifting the saddle forwards and sliding it back again, then doing the girth back up, which will relieve any pressure there may have been on the horse's back; and we always leave it on as this helps to keep the back muscles warm.

'The horse is then washed down and towelled off as quickly as possible – we wash the head and mouth, the neck and chest, the girth area, around the stomach and up between the hind legs, but we don't put any water over the loins or hindquarters in case this causes cramp in those muscles. How much washing is done depends on the weather, but it should be performed quickly. We always use a plastic sweat scraper as this is gentler on tired or sore muscles, and then towel off afterwards. Avoid leaving water on the coat as this will warm up again quickly and will prevent the horse cooling down properly. Put a sweat rug or, if it is cold, something more substantial over the hindquarters.

'We do offer the horse a few mouthfuls of water, and also sponge his mouth out really well. Then we squirt glucose water and glycerine from a big syringe into his mouth; the glucose water refreshes him and the glycerine helps keep the mouth moist – if the mouth gets very dry the tongue can flip back and block the airway once he starts galloping again. He is then led around quietly, although we are careful that he is not asked to stop or turn too sharply as he could easily knock himself or twist a joint at this stage. Once five minutes are up we put the cross-country grease on, making sure that it doesn't get on to any of the tack; the time-keeper will keep you informed of how much time you have left. I like to be back on board, and girthed up with two minutes to spare.

Steeplechase kit

(which is also brought back to the ten-minute box)

Spare shoes and studs

Spare bridle, stirrup and leather, spare girth

Bucket and sponge

Boots, bandages and tape

Stud kit

Bottle of water

'As regards tack, we always carefully position the overgirth so that the buckle lies directly underneath the stomach. If it is to one side the horse may rub his elbows on it, or it may rub the rider's leg. Our ordinary girths have leather loops stitched to them so that the overgirth can pass through these and is held securely in place; if it slips off to one side it will pinch the horse and he may be too sore to take a saddle the next day.

'Time passes very quickly in the ten-minute box so it is important to be organised and to be sure that everyone knows exactly what they are meant to be doing. And if something does go wrong it is important that you don't panic, because there is really nothing you can do about it: the problem will either be sorted out, or it won't. It is essential to keep a cool head for everyone's sake, the horse, the helpers and yourself, because if things resolve themselves you still need to be in a fit state to give your horse a fair ride round Phase D, the cross-country course. Attention to every detail before any event will help avert most problems: check the stitching and buckles on all tack; make sure the horse has been shod fairly recently; and check all his shoes thoroughly the day before so that if a clench is rising or the shoe is slipping it can be dealt with *before* the day itself.'

AZOTURIA (TYING UP)

'One particular problem that can occur at a three-day event is that the muscles over the horse's loins and quarters cramp up; this is a condition known as azoturia, and is usually caused by inefficient feeding – generally when the horse is given too much high protein feed for the amount of work he is doing. Although not a common problem, it is serious enough that every rider should be aware of it, and should do his best to manage his horse in such a way that he is not affected by it. Some horses – and in my experience mares in particular – are more prone to azoturia than others, but in general it can be avoided by awareness and good management. If the horse is going to "tie up" it is most likely to happen either on Phase C, in the ten-minute box, or at the end of the cross-country phase. In its early stages the horse starts to take shorter steps behind, and he will gradually get stiffer and stiffer. If this happens on Phase C you will need to stop the next rider coming up behind you, and ask him to send someone back to help; and it is essential that *you* stop, too, as you can do more damage by trying to keep the horse going. The person who comes back to help you should first inform the vet and tell him where the horse is, and

should bring rugs to keep the horse warm until the vet gets to you.

'Taking the right precautions in the first place, however, should enable you to avoid the problem: don't feed too much protein in the diet, always warm the horse up properly before asking him to do anything strenuous, and keep him warm after he has exerted himself.'

PHASE D – THE COURSE

'The **Quarry** is the first major problem on the course and in 1994 it proved very influential, with nine refusals, three falls, and four retirements or eliminations. The jump in is a wall with a drop and a steep slope down into the quarry floor, then competitors run along the bottom of the quarry, coming out the other side over a big stone-wall corner, which was placed just beyond the top of a short, steep bank. The approach to this sort of combination needs to be in a strong, controlled canter, similar to that for jumping into a coffin, but with a little more pace. It needs determined riding, as the horse is quite likely to want to stop because he cannot see where he is going to land. But too much pace will result in too big a jump in, and this could cause the horse to peck or fall on the downhill landing. Horton Point (pictured) produced a bigger and more exuberant jump than was

required, with the result that he landed in a bit of a heap right at the bottom of the bank; horse and rider look as if they might hit the ground, but Mark Todd has kept a superb position – his bodyweight is back behind the horse, his weight is down in his heels, and having slipped the reins to give the horse the freedom he needed to jump, he has kept the contact which he now uses to support the horse and get him back on his feet.

'He succeeds in picking the horse up and getting him off his forehand, and then sends him forwards to the corner wall: horse and rider are focussed on the bank and the jump at the top. Mark rides him positively up the bank so that the lip of the bank gives the horse a good take-off point, and they have a comfortable, safe jump over the wall; this will immediately have helped to restore the horse's confidence, if it had been dented at all.

(continued on page 138)

▲

'The second sequence of pictures shows how much easier it is for the horse if he just pops in over the wall and lands halfway down the bank; like this he can land and then just keep running to the stone-wall corner, and in so doing reduces the risk of anything going wrong. The second picture shows the horse taking a whole stride to the bottom of the bank, which is where Mark and Horton Point actually landed.

'When walking the course this is the sort of thing a rider has to be mentally preparing himself for. He knows he will have to ride quite strongly to the wall, and that this may mean he gets a very big jump in, in which case he must be ready to deal with its unbalancing effect so that he can get to the other side and out without mishap. Straightaway this is what makes Badminton different; a lesser rider than Mark Todd may not have been able to prevent his horse crumpling up on landing – and another year even this winning combination may not be so lucky – they may not find the same footing and could fall. But Mark is a thinking rider: he was prepared for what might happen, and reacted properly.

'The **Keeper's Brush** which comes next, is a typical Badminton 'rider-frightener', although to most horses and riders at this level the fence is something of a let-up even if the spectators think it looks spectacular. Nonetheless, it must still be attacked with determination and with the horse off his forehand and going forwards; but with experience, more and more riders no longer worry about jumping fences of this size, and so the 'rider-frightener' no longer has such a psychological effect.

'In 1994 the **Little Badminton Drop** involved a big drop down followed by a stride to an arrowhead, and the real key to jumping it successfully was how well the rider knew his horse; this influenced how much pace and impulsion he used to get the horse to go off the drop. The choice was to come down either to a strong trot, or a very collected canter; if he came back to a walk there was a real risk that the horse would hesitate, or worse, refuse at the edge of the drop. A drop of this size is going to push any horse onto his forehand,

▲

and there was very little room to pick him up and help him take the stride to the arrowhead; the horse needed to have sighted the arrowhead before he came down the drop, and if both horse and rider could focus on, or beyond, the arrowhead then it was easier to pick the horse up when he landed and ride him to the fence. What you didn't want was the horse to launch off the drop and land in a heap in the bottom, and then when he looked up, suddenly to find himself confronted by another fence he hadn't realised existed; like this he might panic and try to escape the situation by stopping or running out.

'In the photo sequence the horse has trotted to the lip of the drop, the rider has started to stretch his arms forwards as the horse starts to look down over the drop, but has maintained the contact so that the horse has to stay straight and cannot escape the drop by swinging left or right. With the rider in this position – his seat in the saddle, his lower leg on the girth, and his arms allowing the horse freedom – the horse is almost guaranteed to go,

which he does. The result is a very controlled jump off the drop, so the horse has stayed straight and has taken his one stride and jumped the arrowhead. The rider has got jolted forwards, but with a drop of this size that is almost unavoidable; he is also gripping a little with his knees, but again, with a fence like this, once you get into it you just get through it as well as you can manage. He has recovered his position to give them both a comfortable jump over the arrowhead.

'The **Beaufort Bars**: a slightly ascending triple rail placed just on the ledge of another bank, so that it had a downhill approach and also quite a drop on landing. In the picture sequence the fence is ridden very well: the rider has balanced the horse on the approach and all the way to the fence, keeping her lower leg on and her upper body back, and she maintains quite a strong contact to keep the horse's poll elevated.

'Over a fence like this it is important to follow the contact and fold the upper body on take-off, but it

▼

is also vital to keep the lower leg forwards, and to be quick to sit up and get the shoulders back as the horse starts to come down over the fence. Staying forwards with the horse will load too much weight onto his forehead, which will make it hard for him to pick himself up after the impact of landing. The force of the landing will jolt the rider forwards and then back – something similar to the whiplash effect when a car breaks hard – and if his upper body is already too far forwards he can be unseated or, at best, will be less able to support and help the horse. As the last picture shows, it was a big drop to negotiate.

'Badminton is all about thinking the whole way round, and it was at this fence that Mark Todd opted for the fractionally longer route, which involved jumping the rails off to one side where there was less of a drop. Horton Point had taken quite a jarring when he over-jumped at the quarry

which would have been compounded by having also taken the direct route at the Little Badminton Drop, and Mark obviously decided that it was wiser not to inflict further strain on the horse's legs at this fence, and thereby restore his confidence, which he did without losing too much time. If they hadn't had such a big jump at the quarry he would probably have thought nothing of jumping through the middle here, but as I said, Badminton is about thinking your way round as well as riding your way round.

'The **Lake** is always a popular viewing point for spectators, and it never fails to give plenty of spectator sport! In 1994 the jump in was over a bounce of upright rails, and it was the sort of fence which required an extremely bold horse – horses could not afford to back off it at all, otherwise they failed to make the distance through the bounce. The

approach needed to be controlled but very strong – stronger than you would ever imagine you would need to approach a bounce. If it is the horse's first Badminton he has probably never experienced anything as big or daunting as this, and the Lake is intimidating to even the best horses.

▲ 'In the first sequence of pictures the horse has started to back off as he nears the fence. The rider has sat down and looks to be riding him as hard as possible, but despite this he breaks into a trot in front of the first rail. The rider keeps kicking and the horse jumps the first element, but he fails to cover enough ground to be able to bounce out; he tries to fit in a stride and inevitably ends up too close to the second element to take off. He opts to stop, which was probably more sensible than trying to jump it, because they would almost certainly have fallen. It looks as if this horse was simply over-awed by what he saw: the rider did everything she could, but at the end of the day, the horse is bigger and stronger than any of us and even the boldest and the best horses can be a little stunned by the Lake at Badminton – it is probably the biggest expanse of water, and the largest crowd, that they are ever likely to be faced with. Only experience teaches them to deal with it.

'In the second sequence of pictures the difference in the horse's approach is obvious straightaway: he is on a longer stride and is evidently happy to keep moving confidently up to the fence, and just by looking at him it is quite obvious that *this* horse is going to jump. He jumps in well, and is focussed on the second element; he lands much further into the bounce than the previous horse, and so as long as the rider stays behind the movement he will progress easily through the bounce and into the water.

▼

'Leaving the Lake involved jumping up onto a step and bouncing over a gondola; this fence had a big spread to it, but at least there was plenty there to aim at and attack. The previous year the bounce was an arrowhead, and some riders failed to attack it enough because they were more concerned with holding their line to it. Having landed in the Lake horse and rider had to swing left-handed to the exit, so it was important to balance the horse quickly and get him facing in the right direction so that he could see what he had to do next and could keep moving forwards to it. A good, forward jump up the step was needed, and as long as the rider gave the horse the freedom to do this he generally tackled the

gondola successfully. There were between four and five strides from where the horse landed in the lake to the step, though it seemed to ride best for those who landed in balance and were able to turn and ride forwards for four strides to the step. For those who landed in a muddle in the lake, and who perhaps had to stop and turn back on themselves to get their line, the gondola then became an influential fence as there was very little room to build up enough forward impulsion if you had to create this from a standstill. With a big jump like this out of water, the aim always should be to land and to keep the forward momentum through the turn and up to the step.

The **Deer Park Hollow** was another influential fence in 1994 and there was much critical discussion about the apparent inability of some riders to approach this fence with controlled impulsion: there was a tendency to over-ride it which resulted in the horse becoming too flat, and this led to a number of falls and refusals. It was a long, long gallop from the Lake to this fence, and on the last turn as you came to jump it, it was important to make a definite effort to collect and balance the horse, as he was likely to be somewhat flat and 'strung out' and on his forehand. On walking the course it was clear that sufficient determination and forward impulsion was required on the approach to get over the first hedge, but you didn't want to jump in so big that the horse landed too near, or even in, the ditch. Ideally he needed to land over the first hedge, put in a little stride and pop over the ditch, and then go for one stride up to and over the final hedge. It is easy to discuss in theory how to jump this sort of fence, but in fact on the day it came down to how the horse felt as he came round the corner to the fence: if in this sort of situation the horse starts to back down, a rider will suddenly find himself riding much more strongly than perhaps he had intended – but the first priority is to get in over the first element.

'The horses were unable to see the ditch until they took off over the first hedge, and as the first sequence shows, the result is that the horse very often tries to brake suddenly as he lands over the fence. Here, this has given him the room to pop in the little stride before the ditch, but coming in with such forward momentum followed by the horse suddenly trying to anchor up, makes it very hard for the rider to stay behind the movement; the forward momentum and the forces of gravity actually carry the rider forwards much faster than the horse is travelling. It is a bit like a car crashing into a wall – the car stops, but the passenger gets thrown through the windscreen. In the second and third pictures, as the horse lifts his head and shoulders to jump the ditch the rider gets pushed back into the saddle, and she then sits down and rides the horse up the bank and out over the final element.

▲

'The second sequence shows what happens when a horse comes in with too much forward impulsion. The rider is my brother Graham and he is sitting down and really driving the horse forwards on the approach; maybe as he came off the corner he felt the horse take too much of a look at the first element and so he has had to sit down and attack it more than he would have liked. This was the first time Graham had ridden this horse across country, and as they had already had a stop on the course, he may have been playing safe and riding with more strength and determination than he would have done on a horse he knew better; he is sitting down and driving with everything he has got, with the result that the horse jumps in with equal force! However, Graham has anticipated this and has kept

his weight well back, slipped the reins, and kept his lower leg on firmly so that the horse has to keep moving forwards; if you like, this is a rider who has anticipated the "car hitting the wall" and has braced himself against the impact.

'The horse has picked up and bounced over the ditch, but he has landed into the face of the bank which this time does halt his forward momentum.

But again Graham has kept his weight back, his leg is driving the horse forwards, and he has slipped the reins so that the horse can use his head and neck to help lift himself up the bank. Just in front of the hedge the horse is still down on his forehand and so Graham uses the reins to help pick the horse off the floor so that his front end comes up enough to clear the fence.

'The **Sigma Bridge** came next, and it was a very big fence as the "bridge" was built diagonally over the ditch; this meant that the ditch and fence had to be jumped at an angle. The approach was off a corner, so a rider had to turn back on himself to get his line to the fence – then there was very little room to pick up any pace to the jump. He had to be able to balance the horse through the corner, but also keep him moving forwards the whole time, so that he could accelerate to the fence as soon as he came out of the turn. He couldn't afford to let the horse lose impulsion at all through the turn, and when he came out of the corner he just had to hope that he could see a good distance to the fence as there was little room to make any adjustments.

'On the approach to the bridge Matt Ryan is sitting deep into the saddle and riding the horse forwards all the way up to the lip of the ditch; on the point of take-off he has given the horse a slap with the stick to give it an extra thrust of energy so that it will jump up and out over the big spread. He has brought his lower leg well forwards as a safety precaution should the horse fail to make the spread, or peck on landing. Even so, he has given it maximum freedom over the fence so it can use itself fully in its effort to stretch across to the landing side.

'The **Vicarage Pond** is an easier version of the jump into the Lake; the rails are smaller and on more level ground, the distance is a stride rather than a bounce, there is less of a drop into the lake, and less to look at in terms of water and crowds. The fence should not cause a problem unless the horse had a fright at the Lake, or was very tired. It needed the same approach as the Lake, but there was a greater safety margin because the stride distance allowed more adjustment to be made depending on how the horse jumped in over the first element.

'The picture shows the horse about to exit over a natural bank out of the water. This looks easy, but it is the sort of thing that the rider cannot afford to underestimate just because it isn't flagged as a fence. It is a natural hazard, and if the horse is going too fast or is blinded by the spray, then he may just trip up it and unseat the rider. Although it isn't flagged, it is still in the penalty zone and so a fall would incur sixty penalties as well as time faults. As is always the case at Badminton, "it's not over 'till it's over!"

'The **First Luckington Lane Crossing** involved jumping over a dome-shaped bank, the Pimple, into the lane, followed by a stride up onto a bank and off over some rails and a drop. However, having watched the competition throughout the day, it soon became obvious that a stronger and more definite approach to the Pimple was needed than I had thought necessary when walking the course. One of the advantages of riding later in the day is that you benefit from the feedback from earlier competitors, and where this fence did cause problems was if the horse caught a toe on the Pimple. This in fact happened several times, and it is possible that the horses could not judge the shape of the dome and

took it as an upright, or they may have had their minds more on the next bank and rail and just started to put down in front a fraction early. The result was that they tripped as they landed, and then had to fit in two strides across the lane, which brought them very close to the face of the bank. They then just popped up on the bank, and didn't always have enough impulsion to pick up again straightaway to jump off over the rails. So, on reflection, a clean jump in over the Pimple was the key to making the rest of this easy, and this meant coming in with a bit more pace than at first seemed necessary.

The first sequence shows Mark Todd and Just An Ace. The horse is balanced and focussed and Mark is sat in behind the horse looking ahead, with his lower leg squeezing the horse forwards. They get a lovely neat jump in and Mark is then in a perfect position to ride the horse up to the bank; his weight is back, his lower leg well forward, he is looking up and ahead and has maintained the contact to keep the horse straight and balanced. They have taken a stride across the lane but have still ended up quite a long way of the bank. Mark has used the contact to help lift the horse off the ground, so that he is not tempted to chip in another stride, and the result is a successful jump out and off the bank.

The second horse has made a much higher jump over the Pimple, and has consequently landed a lot steeper than Mark's horse. The rider has given the horse plenty of freedom so as not to restrict him, but this has left her a bit vulnerable as they land in the lane. She has very little rein contact and her horse could easily have run out, but she has sat down and ridden very positively towards the bank; the horse finds room for two strides which brings him to a closer take off point at the bank where he throws a lovely jump up on it. Because of this horse's particular jumping style – high but very neat – he still has room on top of the back to pick up again and jump out over the rails.

'The **Zig–Zag** is another of those big, bold, rider-frightener fences that we have talked about before – and this horse and rider show that it really holds little fear for competitors at this level. At a one-day event this would be a very sizeable fence, but at a big three-day like Badminton, if the horse is fit enough and still full of running, it does not pose a problem. When the course is ridden in the opposite direction, however, it is more of a challenge as it comes early in the course when horse and rider may still not quite have settled to their task.

'The **Three Diamonds** was one of the last combinations on the course; the direct route here was a bounce, then a stride to another bounce of slightly angled rails. One of its problems was that it was late in the course; by this stage any horse would be a little tired and, having galloped so far, more on its forehand than usual. If a rider was confident that he could take hold of the horse, lighten its front end and, most important of all, still manage to keep the engine running, then the fence itself was no more than a simple grid. It all depended on how tired the horse was, and how it would react to being picked up at this stage and asked for more engagement and impulsion.

'In the first picture Rodney Powell is starting to ask his horse to elevate his front end, so that he can then ride him forwards to the fence with plenty of impulsion. The horse must move up into the bridle so that he comes off the floor with the lightness and energy that this fence dictates. Having jumped through the first bounce successfully, with the rider in balance with the horse, the rest should follow through easily. However, if a rider felt his horse might find it all a bit of an eyeful, or if it was very tired, then it was better that he rode the alternative, because as soon as a horse backs off a fence like this, or leaves a leg, or even just toes one of the rails, it will lose its rhythm and impulsion and will struggle to get through.

▼

▲

'The alternative was to jump one corner, then to pull up and turn back at a right-angle to jump a second corner. The corners themselves were straightforward enough, but the inherent risk in this route was that a rider wouldn't attack the first corner sufficiently because of having to pull up and turn almost immediately upon landing. Nor could he afford too big a jump over the first element otherwise he would not be able to turn to the second corner without crossing his tracks. The second problem here was that this sharp turn really had to be made without using too much hand; if the horse was hauled around with the hand he would resist and throw his head up, and would therefore not be focussing on the second corner soon enough to jump it successfully. But if you could pull up and turn smoothly back to the second element then it was a fairly straightforward fence.

'Graham is shown taking the alternative route, and the crucial stage of riding this combination is shown in the third picture, where he has to stop and turn sharp left: the horse is just thinking about objecting and throwing his head up, which would risk him losing his line to the second corner. But by easing off the rein and pushing the horse's quarters round with his lower leg Graham keeps its shape and its concentration so that by the next picture they are in unison again.

'The **Children with Leukaemia's Sunken Road** was the next question, and although it was straightforward enough it did come late in the course, and so the priority was the same as at the Three Diamonds – to collect and engage the horse's hind end, and to make sure he was concentrating on the fence. It involved a jump in over a log pile, then a bounce down into the bottom of the road, one stride across it, before bouncing out over another log pile. The same determined but contained approach that was called for at the Deer Park Hollow was needed here. The horse wouldn't see the sunken road until he was about to take off over the log pile, so sufficient impulsion was needed to be sure he wouldn't stop. If you came in with sufficient control, and were able to hold your line, the distances were very fair and kind to the horse.

'Now all that remained was the **Stick Pile**, which although of maximum dimensions, is a straightforward fence. But as I stressed when talking about the last mile of the course at Gatcombe, a tired horse needs keeping together and coaxing along, even when approaching a let-up fence.

'The slight turn to the final fence, the **Mitsubishi Gardens**, prompted the rider to re-balance and engage his horse on the approach to one of the most welcome sights an event rider can ever hope to see – the finish line!'

Care after the Cross-Country Phase

Leslie points out that the 'after-care' of the event horse actually starts *before* the rider dismounts at the end of the course: 'It is important to remember the importance of pulling the horse up gradually after he has galloped for the finish. Asking him to pull up sharply, or making a sharp turn with him at this stage, is highly likely to result in a leg strain of some sort. As you come through the finish you should be aware of how much room has been allowed for you to pull up; bring the horse carefully back to a canter, then into a trot and then to walk, ideally on a straight line if room allows. The rider should then dismount, run up the stirrups, and undo the girth, safety girth and noseband. The horse is then led back to the lorry by which time he should have stopped blowing. We untack quickly, wash the horse off completely, and then sweatscrape and towel dry him. The horse is offered small drinks of water. While he is being washed down he is checked over for any cuts, or knocks, and these are treated immediately. A sweat rug is put on, plus further rugs if it is cold but always an extra rug over the loins. When the horse is sufficiently

recovered he is allowed to pick at some grass. If the going was hard then we put Ice Tight on the horse's legs. Stable bandages are always put on anyway, and left on until the following morning. Bandages should not be put on too tightly in case any swelling does occur. Once the horse is dry and settled he is put on the lorry and usually given a haynet, or his feed, depending on the time of day.

'It is even more important at a three-day event to be aware of pulling up slowly and carefully after the cross-country phase. The saddle may have to be removed immediately so that the rider can weigh in, but either way the priority is to get the tack off and walk the horse round quietly if he is blowing hard. Once his breathing has settled a bit we would wash him off, scrape and towel him dry, again making a careful check for injuries of any kind. Depending on how close the stables are, and on how settled or otherwise the horse is, we may decide to do all the washing down and so forth back at the stables rather than in the ten-minute box. After the horse has been allowed some water and a quiet graze, we put ice on the legs for about fifteen

minutes. We then apply Ice tight and stable bandages and return the horse to his stable to relax. We generally lead him out later to help walk off any stiffness, but beyond that I like to leave my horses in as much peace as possible so that they can rest. At six o'clock that night we trot them up to check they are sound, and let them have a graze before putting them away for the night. If any horse is lame we get the vet to have a look so that we know what we are dealing with. If it is bruising there is a chance that more ice treatment may put it right, but if it is anything more than that there is no point still trying to get the horse right for the following day. We would follow whatever treatment the vet recommends, and would withdraw the horse from the showjumping phase. The present rules do not allow you to give the horse any drugs at all to help reduce bruising or pain. However, we always give our horses arnica, which is a homoeopathic treatment which can help reduce bruising in particular. On the morning of the trot up I usually hack the horses out for twenty minutes or so to help loosen them up before the vetting, and to reassure myself that they are fit to be presented.'

Hugh Thomas

BADMINTON

Hugh Thomas is an experienced course designer and the director of Badminton Horse Trials; he has very definite objectives in view when designing a course: 'When designing a cross-country course, *some* of my objectives are quite unrelated to the level I am designing for; they include trying to make the course fit as naturally as possible into the surrounding countryside, and using materials indigenous to the area so that they, too, will blend in. All this, of course, has to be balanced with the budget that is available. I like to use the terrain in an interesting way and to its best advantage, though without going over the top – things which are of little relevance to the horse but are usually appreciated by riders and spectators.

'Generally I believe that every course should have a beginning, a middle and an end. At any level the beginning should aim to get horses and riders going fluently; the most difficult part of the course should be in the middle, and the end should be slightly harder than the beginning. In practice, however, the terrain does not always allow this to work quite the way you would like.

'Cross-country course designers have two main objectives: to educate the horse and/or his rider, and to test them, and at every level they will try to fulfil both but in different proportions. Thus in Pre-Novice the main aim is to educate, although certain basic questions must still be asked, such as will the horse jump ditches, will he trot into water, and so on; and it is always desirable that competitors finish having learnt something which will prepare them for when they move up to the next level. The course must also be sufficiently testing so that those who are really not capable of upgrading are prevented from doing so. Just building twenty easy fences doesn't teach anything to anyone, but horses and riders are educated if invitingly, shaped fences are included which incorporate ditches, drops, water, in-and-outs and suchlike.

'At the highest level the principal objective is to test the ability of the horse and rider, because by the time they get to, say, Badminton, they should be well educated. The test must not, however, be so severe that even the horses that succeed are dispirited by having undertaken it; and this is why relatively straightforward fences are incorporated, and why such importance should be placed on the flow of the fences, and the balance of the questions throughout the course. The average horses should finish happy as well as the best; they may pick up some penalties, but they should not come to any harm. Inevitably at this level, however, some people will still fail the test, which is why I, personally, like to ask quite serious questions reasonably early on in the course so that the truly incompetent horse and rider partnerships are stopped. It need not be a technical fence – usually a good "rider-frightener" with a decent ditch and spread is sufficient.

'When designing at Novice level, a course builder should only ever ask one question at any one fence or combination; thus, if he were trying to see how well competitors could turn between fences, then he should make sure the two fences used were straightforward – he shouldn't try and test this particular ability through a coffin fence or in water. The classic question of, say, water, should at this stage only ask of the horse to jump into it, and not, for example, to jump a bounce in. When a bounce is included it should be somewhere on the course on good ground and with a nice approach.

'At the highest level, however, a designer may well want to ask two or three different questions within one fence or combination. Personally I think that Intermediate and ordinary Advanced classes are the hardest levels to design for: because the balance between "testing" and "educating" alters as you go up through the grades, it is hard to get this middle section just right. At the highest level the designer is inevitably walking a bit of a tightrope – if he is over-cautious he won't provide a testing enough course, and if he goes over the top then even the best horses will struggle with it.

'Whether or not a course builder decides to alter a track greatly from one year to another does depend to some degree on whether the event is being run purely for the benefit of competitors, or whether the intention is to attract a large number of spectators, the press, television coverage and so on. If the event is an ordinary one-day event, then I think some courses get changed more than is necessary, particularly at Novice level. Here, you would not expect the majority of riders to return year after year on the same horses, because they should have upgraded by then, and there is no point in changing a good, educational course just for the sake of change.

'At the other end of the scale, however, at Advanced standard and particularly at three-day events of three- and four-star level, the same horses do often return year after year, and spectators and riders look forward to seeing what's new on the course. I think people like to see a mix of new ideas as well as the traditional fences. I never want to lose the traditional sites at Badminton such as the Quarry, the Lake and the Luckington Lane crossings, but I do believe there is always room for change and innovation elsewhere throughout the course.

'When designing any course it is tremendously important constantly to look at it as a whole, rather than as twenty separate fences – these are all inter-related, one to another and with the terrain, and with how the horse is feeling at each stage of the course. The following experience of mine exemplifies this: at one particular Badminton in the eighties we had all walked the course and felt very confident about riding it, because although it included a great many "question" fences, they were all familiar – we had all either ridden them in previous years, or had seen them ridden by others. However, this particular Badminton cross-country course caused more trouble than anyone had expected because the effect of having to jump all these fences *within one course* had not been fully appreciated; a great many of us had unexpected penalties. Thus a designer should not ask too many questions – no matter how familiar they are – within the same course.'

THE 1994 BADMINTON COURSE

'There are two things which always influence the difficulty of the course at Badminton: the ground, which is fairly flat so that in good conditions Badminton is less of an endurance test than, say, Burghley; and secondly, the route of the cross-country course which, although it can be run in both a clockwise and an anti-clockwise direction, will always stay broadly the same – the course works well over this route and it uses the best ground in the park.

'My current philosophy is to encourage as many riders as possible to tackle the direct routes on the course. I don't want these to be so hard that only the Olympic champion jumps them, I want to encourage bold and attacking riding (with discretion) from the average rider at the event. To this end the direct routes may have become a little easier, taking the course as a whole, than those I would have designed five years ago.

'For the 1994 course the first real change I made came at **Huntsman's Close** (fences 3 and 4), where I put in a pair of upright gates followed by a shortish turn to a big trakehner. If the horse was well ridden, and was reasonably bold and experienced, then he made nothing of either of these. Nevertheless a few stopped at the trakehner or jumped it very badly, and this exonerated my policy of asking an early "question" in order to stop those that, although they have qualified, are really not up to the test.

'The **Quarry** (fences 5 and 6) is such an attractive feature of the park that I will always try to use it – by this time the horses have gone about a kilometre and so the track can start to ask questions of them. At this stage in any course, although the question may be serious, to my mind it should always be something that requires the horse to keep going forwards and straight; so, at this early point in the course I would not want the direct route here to involve a lot of turns or the need to check the horse right back.

'The **Keeper's Brush** is straightforward, and takes competitors on to the **Little Badminton Drop** (fence 8): this is one of the few places in the park where the terrain is unusual, and so I always put a fence here which makes the most of that. The idea of the drop to the arrowhead was taken from a fence used at the European Championships the previous year; the terrain here is different, however, and so although it is in essence the same fence, it is not as big a test as was asked at the Championships.

'The **Beaufort Bars** (fence 9) were very straightforward, sloping rails with a drop on landing. They were a late change to the plan of the course; originally I had wanted to use the Beaufort Steps which had featured in previous courses, but as the Lake came next, that would have meant three testing fences together.

'The **Lake** (fences 11 and 12) at Badminton is always a severe test: it is easy to underestimate the effect of the huge crowds that gather round the Lake, and as designer, it would be easy to overdo the severity if you were not careful. The route across the actual lake involves a relatively narrow stretch of water, and this means that the exit fence is as influential as the one going in because there is so little time to get organised and gathered up again once you have dropped into the water; some riders did not appreciate this and, generally, they were the ones who picked up penalties at the exit over the **Gondola**.

'The **Shooting Butt** (fence 13) is a classic let-up fence, and is simply there to give horse and rider an enjoyable experience. It is followed by the **Deer Park Hollow**; this fence was used in both 1990 and 1992 but for some reason it did not ride nearly so well this year. In many cases it was badly ridden, and this could have been due to over-familiarity; too many riders did not approach it with the degree of collection that it demanded. Equally, however, I am not over-happy with it as a fence because many of the horses that jumped it clear still did not jump it very comfortably. It will almost certainly be significantly different in 1995.

'At the **Sigma Bridge** (fence 15) I was disappointed that more riders did not take the direct route. I can see now that the alternative, when ridden in this direction, was not sufficiently time-consuming to deter riders from using it; even a good many of the top riders took the long route here, which is not what I had intended to happen. In 1993 this fence was jumped from the opposite direction and caused quite a lot of trouble; several horses hit it and there were also some falls. This proved to me that when horses have a downhill approach to a fence they tend to jump too flat. This year those that tackled it had a level approach and a slightly uphill landing and the horses jumped it much better.

'The **Vicarage Vee** (fence 16) is another Badminton classic. The usual fear held by riders trying to take the direct route here is that they will drift too far to the left and land in the ditch on the far side. To encourage more riders to tackle the straight route and to make the fence kinder to the horses, I altered its design from previous years by providing an extra rail which prevented horses from jumping too far to the left. It worked really well in that the fence saw a few stops, but no horses landed in the ditch; so this design will definitely be used again!

'For horses that have got this far and are still going well, the second water at the **Vicarage Pond** (fence 17) is not a difficult test; the rails are not huge and the water is not very deep. Nevertheless it is enough of a question to stop any partnership that is not having a good day, and would hopefully prevent them from struggling on around the course.

'The **First Luckington Lane Crossing** did not jump as well in this direction as I had hoped it would. Quite a few horses clipped the back of the "drum" with their front feet, probably because it was not sufficiently well defined. The drum was gravelly on top, the road was gravel and the face of the bank was stone, and I don't think they could identify clearly enough what they were meant to be jumping. So all this will have to be borne in mind if I use it again in this direction.

'The ground around the **Centre Walk** (fences 20 and 21) is the least good of the whole track and so I never have anything too testing here; the two hedges are intended to be an enjoyable let-up for both horse and rider.

'The farmyard at **Tom Smith's Walls** (fence 22) is an attractive feature of Badminton and the flags are now positioned so that most riders are

encouraged to jump the corner; a few years ago the majority would have taken the alternative. The **Second Luckington Lane Crossing** is a natural road crossing, so it is important not to lose this aspect when designing the fences here. I think it was about right this time: it simply tested the rider's ability to hold his horse on a straight line, having already run and jumped for three-and-a-half miles.

The late Col Frank Weldon (the previous Badminton director) was always telling me that the designer at Badminton must keep finding different ways of jumping over ditches as these are a natural feature of Badminton Park. So the **Zig-Zag** (rails over a ditch) at fence 25 is simply meant to look imposing, but is not intended to cause any trouble.

'When the course has been run in this direction before, people criticised its design for not having quite enough in the last mile to prevent riders from simply sitting down and kicking for home. So I put in two combinations, the **Three Diamonds** and the **Sunken Road**; both of these jump best for those who are prepared to hold a line and just go straight through them. At the **Three Diamonds**, more riders than I would have hoped opted to jump the two corners on a turn rather than go straight through the bounce, stride, bounce combination – which, as Bruce Davidson put it, ". . . was really no more than the sort of straightforward grid exercise you would do at home"; but then, of course, Bruce is a very good rider! For those who did try the "grid exercise", it jumped very well. Of those who took the corners, I suspect they caused more trouble than anticipated. Each corner on its own would have been passed as suitable on an

Intermediate course – but placed on a turn, and at this late stage in the course, some horses objected to being pulled off their line and did not focus soon enough on the second corner.

'The **Sunken Road** which followed was very carefully designed so that the distances were just right for horses to bounce in, take one stride, and bounce out; there was nothing to trick or trap them. However, both these combinations made sure that riders were aware of the need to conserve some energy in their horses to get them safely through. But even though it did ride well, I am still not entirely sure that it is right to have the Sunken Road complex this late in the course, and I shall continue to agonise over it until next time!

'The ground from here to the **Stick Pile** (fence 28) is not good, so I would not wish to build anything else in between; but it does mean that it is quite a long galloping stretch to this fence. The last obstacle, the **Mitsubishi Garden**, was deliberately sited so that riders had to turn to jump it: this made sure that they set their horses up properly, something which would be appreciated by those that were tired, rather than just galloping for home and treating the fence simply as an obstacle in the way of them and the finish.

'At this particular Badminton, about the only thing I regret is that the going was so good that a lot of horses finished inside the time, and this does affect the final result. I was confident that I had measured the quickest possible route, but a few riders claimed afterwards that they had measured a shorter distance than I did – it won't happen again!'

Author's Note & Acknowledgements

They say that eventing is one of life's great levellers: one minute you're celebrating a successful competition, the next you're face down in the mud! This book was written during the 1993 and 1994 seasons, and at the start of 1993 we were full of plans and hopes for our own horses. Leslie was well settled in his new yard with a string of potentially top-class horses and high hopes of producing a serious challenge at Badminton on Haig. I, in a much smaller way, was looking forward to bringing out my six-year-old 'Bear', whom I had had since he was three and who was due to start his eventing career. By the end of 1994, several dreams lay in tatters: Leslie had suffered a broken ankle, which put him out of Badminton, and then just as he got himself back in the saddle ready for a crack at Gatcombe and Burghley, a young novice horse ran into a tree with him at Stowe, knocking him unconscious and damaging his shoulder. Leslie recovered just in time to ride Haig to fifth place at Gatcombe, only for Haig to then bruise a foot and have to be withdrawn from Burghley. My own tragedy was having to have Bear put down due to an untreatable problem with his hock.

Every event rider has moments of utter despair; but the one thing the sport teaches you, at every level, is to pick yourself up and kick on again. There were very many successes for Leslie despite his setbacks, and there will be many more in the future.

I am now looking forward to the new season with two young horses – it has meant starting from scratch, but we'll get there in the end!

Being involved in eventing has taught me a tremendous amount, and the lessons you learn help you in all aspects of life. My greatest thanks go to Martin, who gave me the chance to take up eventing, and who continues to encourage and support me in my hopes and ambitions; to Leslie from whom I have learnt a great deal during the writing of this book; to Sue Williams-Gardner, our photographer; and to Sue Hall our publisher for backing the idea once again.

Leslie: 'I would like to thank Debby for providing the inspiration for this book – it's not something I would have done on my own! Thanks to Harriet, my wife, for her help in every way and for keeping everything going so that I am free to compete; all the people who have helped and trained me, especially Ian Silitch: my family for the support that they continue to give me: and to everyone who has made it possible for us to have our own yard and business, and who continue to support us – the owners of the horses I ride, Hartpury College, Shearwater Insurance and Aubiose (UK) Ltd.'

Index